Studies in the Scriptures

The Epistle to the
Ephesians

THE WEALTH & WALK
OF THE CHRISTIAN

JOHN STEVENSON

© John Stevenson, 2011
All rights reserved
2nd printing 2012

Redeemer Publishing
Hollywood, FL
www.RedeemerPublishing.com

ISBN-13: 978-0982208649
ISBN-10: 0982208642
Dewey 227.5

Unless otherwise noted,
Scripture quotations taken from the New American Standard Bible®,
Copyright © 1960, 1962, 1963, 1968, 1971, 1972, 1973,
1975, 1977, 1993, 1995 by The Lockman Foundation
Used by permission. (www.Lockman.org)

Other books by John Stevenson:

    Doctrines of the Bible: *Outlines in Systematic Theology*
    Ecclesiastes: *A Spiritual Journey*
    Facing the Flames: *A Fire Fighter's Meditations on the
        Spiritual Life*
    First Corinthians: *Striving for Unity*
    Galatians: *Our Freedom in Christ*
    Genesis: *The Book of Beginnings, Volume 1*
    Hebrews: *The Supremacy of the Savior*
    James: *A Faith the Works*
    Joshua, Judges, and Ruth: *Victory, Defeat, and Hope in an
        Age of Heroes*
    Luke: *In the Footsteps of the Savior*
    Mark: *The Servant who Came to Save*
    Preaching from the Minor Prophets
    Romans: *The Radical Righteousness of God*
    A Survey of the Old Testament: *The Bible Jesus Used*

To Paula
my beloved wife,
the one who has walked
this journey
with me throughout
my life

TABLE OF CONTENTS

An Introduction of the Epistle to the Ephesians 1

Introduction and Salutations, Ephesians 1:1-2 7

A Reason for Living, Ephesians 1:3-6 14

Prized Possessions, Ephesians 1:7-14 23

A Prayer for All Seasons, Ephesians 1:15-23 33

From Death to Life, Ephesians 2:1-7 44

Faith & Works, Ephesians 2:8-9 55

A House United, Ephesians 2:20-22 64

The Mystery of Chris, Ephesians 3:1-13 72

Paul's Priestly Prayer, Ephesians 3:14-21 80

The Christian Walk, Ephesians 4:1-16 86

Christological Implications, Ephesians 4:17-24 100

The Right & the Wrong of It, Ephesians 4:25-32 108

Clean Living in an Unclean World, Ephesians 5:1-14 120

Walking in Submission, Ephesians 5:15-21 127

Instructions to Wives. Ephesians 5:22-24 134

Instructions to Husbands. Ephesians 5:25-33 138

Instructions to Children and Fathers, Ephesians 6:1-4 147

Slaves and Masters, Ephesians 6:5-9 150

Spiritual Warfare, Ephesians 6:10-20 155

Final Farewells, Ephesians 6:21-24 168

Bibliography 173

Free Powerpoints of this commentary and others are available on the John Stevenson Bible Study Page at http://JohnStevenson.net

AN INTRODUCTION OF THE EPISTLE TO THE EPHESIANS

The epistle to the Ephesians is divided into two major sections. The first section tells you what you need to know. The second section tells you what you need to do about what you know.

1:1	1:15	2:1	3:1	4:1	4:17	5:17	6:10
Wealth of the Christian				**Walk of the Christian**			
Praise	Paul's prayer	Past vs. present	Paul's prayer	Call for unity	Call for new walk		Call for new armor
Work of God				Walk of the Christian			
Heavenly Standing				Earthly Walk			

The first three chapters describe the wealth of the Christian. Paul speaks seven times of the "riches" and the "inheritance" that we have in Christ.

      1:7   "according to the riches of His grace"
      1:11   "we have obtained an inheritance"
      1:14   "a pledge of our inheritance"
      1:18   "the riches of the glory of His inheritance"
      2:7   "the surpassing riches of His grace"
      3:8   "the unfathomable riches of His grace"
      3:16   "the riches of His glory"

Chapters 4-6 give the walk of the Christian. We are exhorted five times to walk in a proper way (in chapter 6 this is changed to "stand firm").

      4:1   "walk in a manner worthy of the calling with which you have been called"
      4:17   "walk no longer just as the Gentiles also walk"
      5:2   "walk in love"

5:8	"walk as children of light"	
5:15	"be careful how you walk"	
6:11	"stand firm against the schemes of the devil"	
6:13	"stand firm"	
6:14	"Stand firm"	

Ephesians is a letter about the church – the body of Christ. The church is described here as...
- A body (Ephesians 1:22-23;4:4; 4:16).
- A building (Ephesians 2:19-22).
- A bride (Ephesians 5:25-27; 5:32).

PURPOSE OF THE EPISTLE

Given the makeup of the epistle, we can determine that Paul has two primary purposes in writing. These purposes align with the way we have outlined the epistle.

1. To confirm the position that we have in Christ.

2. To describe what should be the corresponding conduct which believers ought to exhibit as a result of that new position.

This means that Ephesians covers the whole realm of grace in the Christian life. It covers grace for salvation and it covers grace for living. These are not unrelated within the book of Ephesus. Indeed, they bear a cause and effect relationship to one another. It is because of the position we have received in salvation that we are to find the motivation to live in a manner that accords with the recipients of that salvation.

The first three chapters will deal with who we are in Christ. They deal with the problem of identity crisis. Only after you find out who you are can you understand how you ought to live. To put this another way, you do what you are. That is antithetical to the popular teaching of the world that says, "You are what you do."

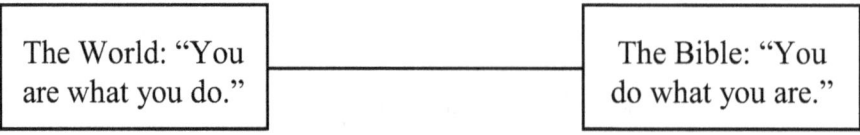

Thus, for the first three chapters of this epistle there will not be a single command given. It will not be until chapter four that we read resulting commands on how we ought to conduct our lives. Paul is going to tell us for the first three chapters who we are in Christ and then he will turn his attention in the last three chapters on what you are to do as a result of who you are.

KEY WORDS

1. *Charis* (Grace): 12 times.

   Charis was used in the ancient world to describe a favor that one did for a friend. But *charis* in the New Testament takes an infinite leap forward. God has shown grace toward us when we were His enemies.

2. *Pneuma* (Spirit): 15 times.
   Pneumatos (Spiritual): 3 times. There is an emphasis within this epistle of spiritual possessions, a spiritual inheritance, and a spiritual war.

3. *Musterion* (Mystery): 6 times. This epistle speaks of revealed truth which had previously been hidden.

GENERAL CHARACTERISTICS

1. There are very few personal notes or biographical references within the book.

2. There is a distinctive style to Ephesians which sets it apart from the other epistles of Paul. There are 42 words which are used here which are not found in any other New Testament book.

3. There are a number of very long sentences within the epistle.
   - Ephesians 1:3-14
   - Ephesians 1:15-23
   - Ephesians 3:1-7
   - Ephesians 3:8-12
   - Ephesians 4:11-16

Most translations have broken these up into several sentences, but in the original Greek text they are one continuous sentence.

4. There are two prayers of Paul recorded in this epistle.
   - Ephesians 1:15-25
   - Ephesians 3:14-21

MOOD

No one reading this epistle would ever guess that Paul was in prison at the time of writing. Indeed, he had spent several years in prison by this time. Paul refers to himself as "the prisoner of Jesus Christ" (Ephesians 3:1). He calls himself "an ambassador in chains" (Ephesians 6:20). However, in each of these references, there is a mood and an atmosphere of victory.

CONTENT

Chapters 1-3	Wealth	The Christian in Christ
Chapters 4-5	Walk	Christ in the Christian
Chapter 6	Warfare	Christ & the Christian versus Satan and his hosts

EPHESIANS IN RELATION TO OTHER NEW TESTAMENT BOOKS

1. Ephesians and the Epistles of Paul.

Romans	Ephesians	1 Thessalonians	1 Timothy
1 Corinthians	Philippians	2 Thessalonians	2 Timothy
2 Corinthians	Colossians		Titus
Galatians	Philemon		
Foundational Epistles	Prison Epistles	Prophetic Epistles	Pastoral Epistles

Introduction to Ephesians

Faith	Love	Hope	Church order
Christ & the cross	Christ & the church	Christ & second coming	Christ & the congregation
Conflict	Conquest	Consolation	Consistency
Soteriology	Christology	Eschatology	Ecclesiology

2. The Prison Epistles.

Four of the epistles of Paul were written while he was in prison. Ephesians is one of those epistles.

Place of Writing: Rome			Date: 61-63 A.D.
Colossians	**Ephesians**	**Philemon**	**Philippians**
Local assembly letter	Circular letter to be distributed	Private personal letter	Local assembly letter
Doctrinal		Ethical	Social
Christ is the head of the church	The Church is the body of Christ	Master and slave	An apostle's gratitude
Christ in all	All in Christ	Christ in the home	Christ in the assembly
Paul's mind		Paul's heart	
Apologist	Theologian	Gentleman	Saint
Discussion	Reflection	Motivation	Friendship
Asia			Europe
Carried by Tychicus and accompanied by Onesimus (Col 4:7; Eph 6:21)		Carried by Onesimus (Philem 12-14)	Carried by Epaphroditus (Phil 2:25)

The first three of these epistles were apparently written and delivered at the same time. In spite of that, there are some major differences.

3. Colossians and Ephesians Compared.

Both epistles were written for the same general purpose – to show the relationship between Christ and his church. They also share many similarities in content and in outline. At the same time, there are some differences between the two epistles in their emphasis:

Colossians	Ephesians
Christ and the Cosmos	Christ and the Church
Emphasis on Christ as the head of the church	Emphasis on the church as the body of Christ
More personal - local	Less personal - lofty
Combats error directly	Combats error indirectly
Tone: Intensity & tumult of a battlefield	Tone: Calmness of surveying the field after victory

Colossians is to Ephesians
what
Galatians is to Romans

INTRODUCTION & SALUTATIONS
Ephesians 1:1-2

Paul, an apostle of Christ Jesus by the will of God, to the saints in Ephesus, the faithful in Christ Jesus (Ephesians 1:1).

Ephesians is an epistle. It is written as a letter. We are used to getting letters mailed to us in an envelope which contains the address and the return address and the stamps. Had it been penned today, the envelope of the letter to the Ephesians might have looked like this:

```
Paul, an Apostle
Imperial Prison
Rome, Itally
```
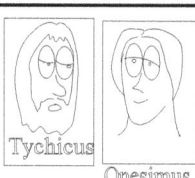
```
           Saints & Faithful Ones
           c/o Elders & Overseers
           Ephesus, Asia Minor
```

Paul is writing from a place of imprisonment, presumably in Rome. He addresses his epistle to the saints and faithful ones in Ephesus. He sends the letter by way of two men, Tychicus and Onesimus (only Tychicus will be mentioned in this epistle, but we see the name of Onesimus included in the parallel epistle to the Colossians).

PAUL

It has been customary to think that Paul changed his name from its original "Saul" to "Paul" so that he could better identify with the Gentiles (Saul is a Hebrew name, while Paul is a Latin name). However, I do not believe that this is completely accurate. In the days in which Paul lived, all Roman citizens had three names.

1. Praenomen: An individual name given at birth. This is the name by which you were known as an individual.

2. Nomen: A tribal name. In Rome there were about a thousand tribes which could trace their ancestry back to a common origin.

3. Cognomen. At first, the cognomen was given as a family nickname, usually referring to some outstanding feature in the individual. Here are a few examples...
   Crassus (Fat)
   Longus (Tall)
   Rufus (red)
   Felix (Happy)
   Paulus (Little)

By the first century, the cognomen had become a family name in the same way people today have a last name. Roman citizens generally possessed three names. Here are a few well-known examples...

- Gaius Julius Caesar
- Publius Cornelius Scipio
- Lucius Sergius Paulus

As you have seen in the above examples, Paulus was a cognomen. It was always used as a cognomen. As such, it was a family name.

Although Paul was a Jew, he had also been born as a citizen of Rome. At some time in the past, it is conceivable that one of his ancestors has been "adopted" into one of the families of Rome and given a Roman name. Thus, when Paul uses this name for himself, he is not making it up. He is merely using one of his names which would serve to better identify himself with the Gentiles.

AN APOSTLE

In addition to the praenomen, nomen and cognomen, the Romans also occasionally used an *agnomen*. This would be a special title of honor and/or authority.

Praenomen	Nomen	Cognomen	Agnomen
Gaius	Julius	Caesar	Imperator
Publius	Cornelius	Scipio	Africanus

Paul also uses an Agnomen. He calls himself an "apostle." *Apostolos* is also the Greek translation of the Hebrew *"sheliach."* A well-known Hebrew proverb states: "The authority of the sent one (*sheliach*) is equal to that of the sender." Thus authority is inherent in the term "apostle" from both its Greek and Hebrew backgrounds.

While the word "apostle" comes from the root verb "to send from" it seems to have a more specific meaning. Indeed, the Greeks of the Peloponnesian Wars used this as a military term for the admiral of their fleet who was "commissioned" with a special duty. When used in this sense, it seems to speak of one who is sent out with special authority. The authority of which he speaks is that which is given to him directly by Jesus Christ – this is the meaning of the phrase "by the will of God."

There is a Hollywood movie called *The Apostle* in which the main character, played by Robert Duvall, baptizes himself as an apostle and thus takes for himself that title. But that was not the case with Paul. He was not an apostle because he decided to become one. He did not appoint himself to be an apostle. His own will did not make him an apostle. He is an apostle "by the will of God."

TO THE SAINTS

To the saints in Ephesus, the faithful in Christ Jesus (Ephesians 1:1b).

When Paul addresses his letter, he is probably not speaking to two different groups of people. It is not as though there were one group who were saints and another group who were faithful. This is a description of the believers at Ephesus. They are described in these two ways. That tells me something about what it means to be a Christian. A Christian is one who can be described in these two ways.

1.   A Saint.

When we use the word "saint" we are inclined to think of a picture on a stained-glass or someone who has been dead a long time. But the Biblical idea of a "saint" is different. The word "saint" comes from the same root as the words "holy" and "sanctify." They all signify the idea of that which is "set apart for a special purpose."

God's people have been set apart. They are special - not because they are so good in themselves, but because the Lord has declared them to be His own special possession. Of course, because He has declared them to be special, He also commands them to be what He has declared them to be.

He says...
   "You are holy!"
   "Now I want you to BE holy!"

What does being holy involve? It involves being "faithful." It involves believing in Christ and seeking to serve Him to whom we have entrusted ourselves.

2.   The Faithful.

This can refer simply to those who are in the process of believing something. We could simply translate it as "the believing ones." Indeed, for the first half of this epistle, Paul is only going to tell the Ephesians to do one thing - to believe what it is that God says about them. But in chapter 4 we shall see a change. In chapter 4 and through the rest of the epistle, we shall see that simple belief brings about a response. It brings about faithfulness. If you really believe, then you will grow in faithfulness.

IN EPHESUS

The words *en Epheso* ("in Ephesus") do not appear in the Chester Beatty Papyrus designated Papyrus 46. This manuscript dates to about 200 A.D., making it the very oldest copy of the Pauline epistles.

While the words do appear in other very old manuscripts, most notably the

Sinaiticus and the Vaticanus, in both cases there are scribal notations in the margin which makes it evident that this reading was not without question. The words also appear in the Alexandrinus.

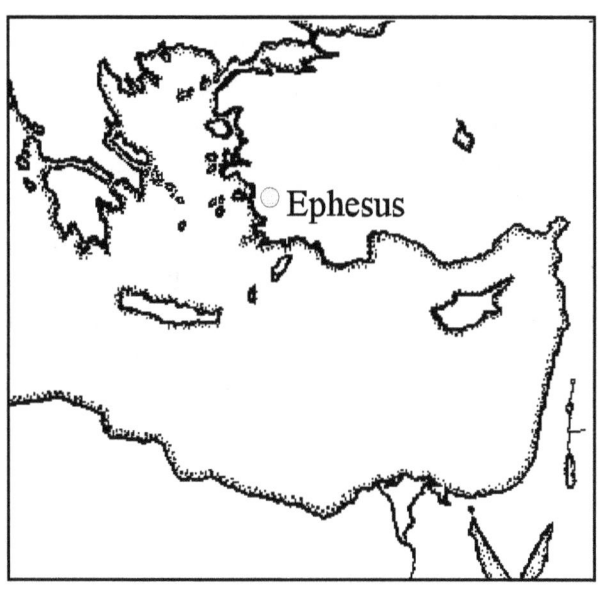

It is possible that, while the epistle was originally written to the Ephesians, it was recognized that the message contained therein had a wider application so that early on it was recopied without the phrase "in Ephesus" and distributed to that wider audience. The city of Ephesus was located at the mouth of the Cayster River on the southwest coast of Asia Minor (modern-day Turkey).

She had been a historic trading city in the past, though recent silt deposits in her harbor were bringing present economic pressures to bear. The harbor would eventually become completely clogged and unusable and the city would ultimately be abandoned.

In Paul's day, Ephesus was the seat of the local Roman proconsul. It was also the center of a pagan cult which was associated with a meteorite thought to have fallen down from the god Zeus (Acts 19). The most significant feature of the city was its temple to the goddess Artemis (Diana of Roman mythology), the fertility huntress-goddess. This temple was said to be four times the size of the Parthenon at Athens, though today only the foundation remains.

The religion of Ephesus reflected both east and west in that it was a mixture of Greek paganism and oriental mysticism.

Paul had first come to this city with Priscilla and Aquila during his second missionary journey (Acts 18:19). After preaching in the Jewish synagogue, he had been invited to remain, but he had declined the offer, continuing instead to Caesarea and then to Antioch. Priscilla and Aquila did remain in Ephesus where they met and discipled a young preacher named Apollos.

Paul returned to Ephesus during his third missionary journey (Acts 19:1) and stayed for a period of three years, teaching daily Bible classes in the school of Tyrannus *so that all who lived in Asia heard the word of the Lord (Acts 19:10).* Paul's ministry was so successful that the silversmith trade which manufactured pagan idols fell sharply. The local idolater's labor union staged a picket line and even went so far as to incite a mob to demonstrate against the Christians, filling the giant theater with protestors in a move that was dangerously close to civil unrest. Paul desired to go and to address the crowd, seeing it as an opportunity to share the gospel, but his companions prevented him, fearing that he would be torn apart by the mob.

Theater at Ephesus

When the uproar had ceased, Paul left for Macedonia to revisit the churches he had planed there. After completing a circuit that took in the churches throughout Greece, he returned to Miletus near Ephesus a final time on the last leg of his third missionary journey. He called for the elders of the church at Ephesus and they traveled to Miletus to meet with him and be exhorted and encouraged by him (Acts 20:17-38). This was his final contact with the church at Ephesus.

PAUL'S SALUTATION

> *Grace to you and peace from God our father and the Lord Jesus Christ. (Ephesians 1:2).*

This was Paul's typical greeting. It was a combination of the typical greetings of the Greeks and the Jews.

- The Greeks would ordinarily say *chairein*, "greetings." This is similar to Paul's greeting of *charis*, "Grace."
- The Hebrews still use as their customary greeting the word *Shalom* - "Peace."

However, I think that Paul's use of these two greetings goes far beyond a mere combination of ethnic greetings. There is a definite order of their arrangement.

Peace always comes after grace. Without grace there can be no peace. Grace is the undeserved favor of God directed toward man. It excludes all human merit. It is the sum total of all that God has done for you.

This is the problem with the world today. The world is seeking for peace without grace. It is only as man meets the grace of God and accepts it that he can find peace with God and then peace with himself and with others.

Paul says that the grace and peace comes *from God our father and the Lord Jesus Christ*. Here is the source of all grace and peace. Note that these are not two separate sources. The Father and the Son are not two separate or competing sources for grace and peace. They are the same source.

God offers His grace and peace to you. If you have never experienced the peace of God, then you can do so today. You can accept the grace of God through faith in His Son.

A REASON FOR LIVING
Ephesians 1:3-6

The old man was nearly blind as he reached out to touch the face and hands of his son. "It is the voice of Jacob, but the hands are the hands of Esau." The aged hands felt the hairy forearms, not realizing that they were wrapped with the skin of a goat to simulate those of his twin brother.

The scene was one of intrigue and deception as Jacob plotted to steal that which his father had allotted to his brother Esau. What was at stake? A plot of ground? A large sum of money? Power? Prestige? No, it was all for a blessing.

We don't normally put so much stock in a blessing. But perhaps we should. Especially when we note how Paul opens his epistle to the Ephesians.

> *Blessed be the God and Father of our Lord Jesus Christ, who has blessed us with every spiritual blessing in the heavenly places in Christ, 4 just as He chose us in Him before the foundation of the world, that we would be holy and blameless before Him. In love 5 He predestined us to adoption as sons through Jesus Christ to Himself, according to the kind intention of His will, 6 to the praise of the glory of His grace, which He freely bestowed on us in the Beloved. (Ephesians 1:3-6).*

When we speak of a blessing, we don't usually talk about blessing God. It is much more common to speak about having been blessed by God. We usually think of the greater one blessing the lesser one – the Lord blessing us. But Paul begins this section by pronouncing a blessing upon both God the Father and upon the Lord Jesus Christ.

The word "bless" is one of the most used religious words among English-speaking Christian people. We use the word constantly in conversation and song:

"Count Your Blessings"
"Bless my soul"
"Showers of Blessing"
"The Lord bless you"

The word is used so much, in fact, that it is often just a buzz word, a cliche. For example, when you say, "The Lord bless you" to someone, are you saying it as a kind of Christian "goodbye"; are you using it as a sort of prayer that the Lord will do good things for that person? Just what is it that you are expecting, or hoping, that the Lord will do?

Or, when you "count your blessings," what are you counting? If you were to list your blessings, would you list all the good things that you might have today, like good health, enough money, happy family life, a job?

But what about the unpleasant things in your life? Are they blessings? Do you think of trials and tribulations, testing, as blessings? If the Lord allows testing of your faith, is that a blessing?

The word "bless" is translated from the Greek term *eulogetos*. It is a compound word, made up from joining two words together.

(1) *Eu* is the word "good."
(2) *Lego* is the verb, "to speak."

The resulting compound means "to speak good toward someone." And that is what Paul is going to do in this chapter. He is going to "speak good" of the Lord. He is going to praise the Lord and exalt His goodness and His power and His grace.

This is important. We tend to be too self-centered in our holding of the Christian faith. "What's in it for me?" Our prayers so often reflect this. We pray as though we were ordering fast food: "I'll have a special prayer request, an order of forgiveness and a couple of blessings to go."

Don't get me wrong. There is a place for requests and supplication. But it is noteworthy that Paul starts by blessing God. It is in this blessing that we will find a motivation to serve.

Why do you serve the Lord? Why do you seek to obey His commands? I want to suggest four reasons. They are taken from this passage.

WE LIVE FOR HIM BECAUSE HE BLESSED US COMPLETELY

Blessed be the God and Father of our Lord Jesus Christ, who has blessed us with every spiritual blessing in the heavenly places in Christ (Ephesians 1:3).

This is not a prayer. Paul is not asking for a blessing from God. Neither is it prophetic. He is not saying that there is coming a day when you will be blessed. Instead, he speaks of a present reality. You have been blessed. It is an accomplished fact (aorist tense). Not only have you been blessed, but you have been blessed abundantly.

> Paul is going to speak in this verse about how we have been blessed by God. But he begins by pronouncing a blessing on God. He blesses God because God has first blessed us.

I occasionally meet Christians who are seeking some sort of "second blessing." What they do not realize is to what extent they have already been blessed. When Paula was a little girl, there was a woman who lived down the street from her who lived in a little dilapidated shack. This woman lived like a pauper, collecting cans and sustaining herself on handouts. When she died, people went into her house and, to their amazement, they found it filled from floor to ceiling with bundles of newspapers. And within each page was a crisp twenty dollar bill. She was wealthy, but she was not living in accordance with her wealth.

We do the same thing when we do not live in accordance with the blessings with which we have been blessed. We live like spiritual paupers when we have been blessed with every spiritual blessing. Why? Because of unbelief. Out of sight, out of mind. And the problem with the realm of blessing is that it is not here on earth where we can see it.

They are Spiritual blessings as opposed to the physical kind. And they are in the realm of the heavenly places versus the earthly places.

Is that bad? No, it's good! Everything physical will pass away. This world on which we live will one day be burned as an old parchment. It is only temporary. But what we have been given is eternal. When the stars have grown cold and the galaxies have ceased their spinning, we will still possess the riches of Christ. They are eternal riches. Because we have an eternal inheritance, we are motivated to make our lives count for today.

But that is not all. Not only have we been blessed. Not only have we been blessed in a realm that is eternal. But we have also been blessed with every spiritual blessing. This includes spiritual gifts, but it is not limited to them. It includes our salvation. It includes answered prayer. And it includes the grace of God for daily living. It includes everything.

Don't miss this! There is no spiritual blessing out there with which you have not been blessed. You are batting a thousand in the spiritual blessing category. They are all yours in Christ.

WE LIVE FOR HIM BECAUSE HE CHOSE US TO BE HOLY AND BLAMELESS

Just as He chose us in Him before the foundation of the world, that we should be holy and blameless before Him. (Ephesians 1:4).

Notice that there is a correlation in the way in which we have been blessed with the way in which we have been chosen.

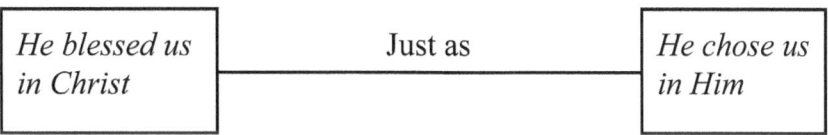

Do you see the correlation? It is that we are *"in Christ."* This is our new position. It is one of union and identity with Christ. We have been united with Him through faith. Because of that union, we have become the recipients of every spiritual blessing with which Christ has been blessed.

> Because He has eternal life, we have eternal life.
> Because He is righteous, we have been declared to be righteous.
> Because He is the king who reigns over all, we have been established as co-heirs with Him.
> Because He is seated at the right hand of God, we have a position in the heavenlies.
> Because He is the holy One of God, we are also said to be holy.
> Because He is without sin, we are also blameless.

We were chosen to be holy and blameless. Holiness and blameless - they point both to our justification and our sanctification.

1. The Greek words for "holy" and "sanctified" and "saint" are all taken from the same root word. The word is *hagios*. Usually we think of the word "holy" as being synonymous with sinlessness. It sometimes carries that idea, but there is more to holiness than mere sinlessness. Holiness describes one who has been set apart for a special purpose. That which is holy is separate and distinct and different and special.

    The utensils in the temple were considered to be holy. They were set apart in a special way and for a special usage. They were no longer to be used for ordinary things. They were now to be extraordinary.

    Remember the time when the apostles were in the boat with Jesus? It had been a long day and Jesus lay down in the bottom of the boat to sleep. The disciples were sailing across the Sea of Galilee and a storm came up. It was a bad storm and when the fishermen among them began to be afraid, it threw the rest of the disciples into a terror. Water was coming into the boat and they were still a couple of miles from land and someone suggested that they wake up Jesus. "I don't want to wake up Jesus, He'll chew us out for our lack of faith." But as the situation gets worse, they wake up Jesus. And He chews them out for their lack of faith. And then He turns to the wind and the waves and says, "Quiet!!!" And the wind and the waves get quiet. And so do the disciples. Because they suddenly realize that the One who has been sleeping in the bottom of their boat is no ordinary man. He is different. He is special. He is holy.

    God has set us apart. He chose us and He called us to be different. We have a special purpose. We have been called to do the King's work and to be His ambassadors. Because of this, we are to seek to live holy lives. We are to live in a way that is set apart from sin and we are to live in a way that is set apart and consecrated unto God.

2. Blameless – without blame.

    God did something special when He saved us. There was a shifting of blame. Our sin and our blame was placed upon Jesus when He hung upon the cross. But that is not all. In the same way that He was credited with our sin and our blame, we were credited with His perfect righteousness.

> *He made Him who knew no sin to be sin on our behalf, that we might become the righteousness of God in Him. (2 Corinthians 5:21).*

It is on the basis of this crediting of righteousness that God declares us to be righteous; He justifies us. That does not mean that we become righteous. It is not on the basis of a certain level of righteousness which is imparted to me. Rather, it is an imputation of righteousness. We are credited with the righteousness of Christ. We are reckoned with a reckoning of righteousness.

That reckoning has some practical consequences. God says, "I have reckoned you to be righteous, now be righteous." It is like the young lieutenant who was called into the general's command post. The general pinned a medal on the young officer and said, "You are a hero. Now go out and lead your men up that hill." In the same way, God says to us, "I declare you to be my holy and righteous children. Now go and live holy and righteously as my own children."

WE LIVE FOR HIM BECAUSE HE HAS DESTINED US TO BE SONS

> *In love He predestined us to adoption as sons through Jesus Christ to Himself, according to the kind intention of His will (Ephesians 1:5).*

The manner by which we came to be sons of God is said to be through adoption. You know about adoption. It is the legal procedure of taking a child that has been orphaned or otherwise abandoned and establishing him as a legal offspring.

> Octavius Augustus was adopted by Julius Caesar in his will. When he learned of this after the death of Caesar, he changed his name, taking for himself the name of his adopted father. While history knows him as Octavius, he was thereafter known to the world as Gaius Julius Caesar. When we come to Christ, we are adopted and given a new name.

They had adoption in the ancient world in much the same manner that we have adoption today. The Greek word translated "adoption" literally means "son-placing." It describes the action of taking someone who was not previously a son and placing him as a member of the family.

We have been adopted into the family of God. He has become our Father. Because of this adoption, we can pray to Him as our Father.

1. Israel had a Similar Adoption.

    In Romans 9:4 Paul is listing the things that belonged to the people of Israel: They have the glory and the covenants and the giving of the Law. And they also have the adoption. God took Abraham and said to Him, "Your family is going to be My family." That is adoption. This means we have entered into a similar covenant arrangement to that which God had with Israel. It is similar, but it is also different. It is a New Covenant. Instead of being written on tablets of stone, it is written in our hearts.

2. This Adoption Casts out Fear.

    For you have not received a spirit of slavery leading to fear again, but you have received a spirit of adoption as sons by which we cry out, "Abba! Father!" (Romans 8:15).

    It is one thing to approach God as a servant coming to a master. It is quite another thing to approach Him as a loving Father. Fear is replaced by love. It is true that some children grow up in fear of their natural fathers, but that is not the way the parent-child relation ought to be. Our Heavenly Father is a perfect father who allows us to come to Him in love.

3. This Adoption is Fulfilled when Christ Comes.

    Notice that this passage says that we have been predestined to be adopted as sons. Being an adopted son makes you an heir. But we have not yet received the fulness of that inheritance.

    And not only this, but we ourselves, having the first fruits of the Spirit, even we ourselves groan within ourselves, waiting eagerly for our adoption as

> *sons, the redemption of our body. (Romans 8:23).*

We still await the full realization of our redemption. We have been redeemed, but that has only impacted soul and spirit. Our outward bodies see no noticeable change when we come to Christ. We may be redeemed, but we don't necessarily look or feel redeemed. But there is coming a time when we will be redeemed on the outside as well as on the inside.

I suffered a heart attack recently. My body came close to dying and, had that happened, it would have been placed in a coffin and buried. But there is coming a day when our bodies shall be changed and when all those who have died will be raised from the dead.

Now I want to make this practical. Because I have been adopted as a son of God, I am now called to live as befits a son. It demands a certain responsibility of me. When she was growing up, our daughter would occasionally ask to partake in something which we felt was not appropriate. The familiar refrain comes to mind: "But all of the other kids are doing it!" And it was at such a time that I would explain to her that I was not the parent of all of the other kids, but that her calling was to live as befit a child of mine.

WE LIVE FOR HIM BECAUSE HE HAS BESTOWED US WITH HIS GRACE

> *To the praise of the glory of His grace, which He freely bestowed on us in the Beloved. (Ephesians 1:6).*

The result of our salvation is that the grace of God is glorified. Grace refers to that quality of unmerited favor; that good gift from above which has been unearned and undeserving.

The word "grace" was a rather obscure word. The Greeks didn't talk a lot about grace. And when they did, they used the term to speak of a favor that one does for a friend. A favor which was unmerited and undeserved and unrecompensed. A kindness for which there was no repayment. A gift.

But God's grace is so much more. His grace was given at a time when we could hardly have been said to be friends. His grace was given when we did not even exist.

Verse 4 says that we were chosen before the foundation of the world. Verse 5 says that we were predestined.

God didn't merely determine the plan of salvation and state, "Whoever trusts Christ and follows me will find himself as one of the chosen and in a predestined place." Election and predestination are personal. He chose us to be the objects of His grace. Why? What motivated God? It was in nothing that we did. We were not there to do anything. He worked *"to the praise of the glory of His grace."*

I have to admit this sounds a bit cold. If we are not careful, we can be so struck with the awesome sovereignty of God that we see only His greatness and His power and His total control of all things to bring about the manifestation of His glory. We should see those things. But that is not all we should see. We should also see His love.

Do you see it? Verse 5 says: *"In love He predestined us..."* And we must never forget that God's election and predestination is rooted in His great and gracious love for us. He loved us to death that we might live His life.

As we have read through this passage, we have been confronted with such heavy subjects as predestination, redemption, adoption, and the sealing ministry of the spirit. The danger is that we might simply analyze these teachings like one discovering a new find at an archaeological dig.

I happen to like archaeology. I also like the study of the minutiae of the Scriptures. But the study of such a text must not remain an academic exercise. It must drive me to worship the Lord, otherwise I miss the entire point. When God reveals to us what He has done for us the proper response is not grab a microscope, but raise my hands heavenward and sing a doxology. All theology is doxology; theology must sing!

PRIZED POSSESSIONS
Ephesians 1:7-14

It was in the spring of 1844 when the young German scholar made a most remarkable discovery. His name was Konstanin Von Tischendorf and he had been traveling through the Middle East. He came one night to an old Greek Orthodox monastery at the foot of Mount Sinai. Knocking upon the door, he was invited in by the Russian monks who lived there and invited to spend the night.

It was bitterly cold in the desert and the monks has baskets of old dry cordwood and vellum to throw into the fire place. Tischendorf was warming his hands at the fire when his eyes caught sight of one of the pieces of vellum and he did a double take. This particular piece of vellum had writing on it. Tischendorf had benefitted from a classical education and he recognized the writing as a part of the Greek Bible. He began digging through the baskets of refuse and came up with 129 pages of what was to be the oldest manuscript of the Bible to be discovered up to that time.

The monks could see that he was excited and they became cautious. When he asked if he could take the manuscript with him, they allowed him to take only 43 of the 129 pages.

The rest of the manuscript was sent to mother Russia where it remained until after the Communist Revolution. It was not until 1933 that the Russian Communists, having no use for old copies of the Bible, agreed to sell the Codex Sinaiticus to Great Britain for a price of 100,000 pounds, one of the most expensive books in the world.

Buried treasure. The term fills us with images of glitter and gold. What is your most treasured possession? Your house? Your car? Some sort of family heirloom? The Lord has a treasured possession. It is you.

> *In Him we have redemption through His blood, the forgiveness of our trespasses, according to the riches of His grace 8 which He lavished on us. In all wisdom and insight 9 He made known to us the mystery*

of His will, according to His kind intention which He purposed in Him 10 with a view to an administration suitable to the fullness of the times, that is, the summing up of all things in Christ, things in the heavens and things on the earth. In Him 11 also we have obtained an inheritance, having been predestined according to His purpose who works all things after the counsel of His will, 12 to the end that we who were the first to hope in Christ would be to the praise of His glory. 13 In Him, you also, after listening to the message of truth, the gospel of your salvation -- having also believed, you were sealed in Him with the Holy Spirit of promise, 14 who is given as a pledge of our inheritance, with a view to the redemption of God's own possession, to the praise of His glory. (Ephesians 1:7-14).

Although it isn't clear from the English translation, the Greek text of Ephesians 1:3-14 is made up of one very long run-on sentence. Paul started this sentence in verse 3 with the phrase: *"Blessed be the God and Father of our Lord Jesus Christ..."* Then he proceeds to tell us what God has done. He does not stop to take a breath, but continues on until the end of verse 14. He cannot stop talking about God. He speaks of all three members of the Godhead.

1:3-6	The Father	Planned our salvation from eternity past
1:7-10	The Son	Accomplished our salvation on the cross
1:11-14	The Holy Spirit	Signed, sealed and delivered us in our new relationship

We are also described in this passage. We are pictured as the recipients of all that God has done.

WE HAVE BEEN REDEEMED

In Him we have redemption through His blood... (Ephesians 1:7).

There are three different Greek words which have been translated for the idea of "redemption" in the New Testament. While they all capture the same general idea, there are slight variations that suggest differing shades of meaning.

1. *Agorazo*: "To purchase."

   When we think of making a purchase, we think of buying groceries or a car or a house or some other inanimate object. We don't talk about purchasing people - that went out with slavery over a hundred years ago. But slavery was commonplace in Paul's day. And you would commonly go into the marketplace - the Agora - to purchase a slave.

2. *Exagorazo*: "To purchase out."

   This is the same word as *agorazo*, but with a prefix placed in front of it meaning "out." The picture is that you go into the slave market and you purchase a slave and then you bring him out of the market.

3. *Lutro'o* or *Apolutrosis*: "To release or set free."

   This is the word used here (*apolutrosin*). It takes the picture one step further as you take that slave that you have purchased and you bring him out of the slave market and then set him free.

   This is what Christ has done for us. He came into this world of sin and He paid the ultimate price for us. It was His own blood shed on our behalf.

   Why is it, *"By His blood?"* Why not merely, "By His death"? I think that the reason blood was necessary was to fulfill the type of the Old Testament sacrifice.

   > It has been argued that a blood sacrifice is primitive and brutal. I agree. But sin is also primitive and brutal and it requires a solution to match.

   Do you remember to story of the Passover? The people of God were enslaved in Egypt. They were in a bitter bondage. Unable to free themselves. And to effect their freedom, God sent 10 terrible plagues against the nation of Egypt. The tenth plague was the worst of all. It was a pronouncement of death. All of the firstborn were to die. Animal and man. Slave and free. Egyptian and Israelite. All were under the sentence of death. There was only one way of escape. It was through the blood of an innocent lamb. A lamb for each household was to be slain and its blood smeared upon the door posts and the lintels of each home.

> *"For I will go through the land of Egypt on that night, and will strike down all the first-born in the land of Egypt, both man and beast; and against all the gods of Egypt I will execute judgments - I am the Lord.*
>
> *"And the blood shall be a sign for you on the houses where you live; and when I see the blood I will pass over you, and no plague will befall you to destroy you when I strike down the land of Egypt." (Exodus 12:12-13).*

Christ has become our Passover lamb. Because of the redemption that we have in Him, God's judgment has passed over us. And as a result, we have been forgiven.

In Him	*We Have*	*Redemption*
Through His blood		*Forgiveness of our trespasses*

WE HAVE BEEN FORGIVEN

> *In Him we have redemption through His blood, the forgiveness of our trespasses (Ephesians 1:7a).*

The fact that we have been forgiven of our trespasses presupposes that there are trespasses of which we are guilty. The fact of our forgiveness presupposes our guilt. That is the bad news. The bad news is that we are guilty. And we don't just deserve a parking ticket. The proper and just wages of our sin is death – eternal separation from God.

The bad news is really bad. But the corresponding good news is really good. It is that Christ took our blame and our guilt and our sin upon Himself. He was the perfect and holy sacrifice for sin. Forgiveness did not come cheap. It never does. Forgiveness always costs somebody something. When someone slaps your face and you forgive, that forgiveness costs you a slap in the face. Our forgiveness cost God the life of His Son. The payment was made at the cross. And because of the cross, we can be assured of total forgiveness.

There is a practical application here. It is that you are to forgive in the measure to which you have been forgiven. To what measure have you been forgiven? Totally!!! It is to that measure that you are to forgive others.

Remember the words of the Lord's prayer? *"Forgive us our debts As we forgive our debtors."* This is the only part of the prayer on which Jesus comments. He goes on to say:

> *"For if you forgive men for their transgressions, your heavenly Father will also forgive you. 15 But if you do not forgive men, then your Father will not forgive your transgressions." (Matthew 6:14-15).*

Here is the principle. Forgiven people forgive. Guilty people try to make other people feel guilty, too. Is there someone for whom you are carrying a grudge? It is to your own hurt. Baggage like that will separate you from appreciating the forgiveness of God. Forgive. And then you will be able to enjoy the forgiveness with which you have been forgiven.

You say, "You don't know how badly I have been hurt. I just can't let go." The answer is to look at the cross. See the One who hangs there, nails piercing his mutilated flesh. See the spittle dripping from His beaten face. The bloody visage that barely looks human. The agonized labor to draw in each new drought of air. And hear His weary voice: "Father forgive them, for they know not what they do." And realize that He was praying, not only for the Roman soldiers who drove the nails, not only for the Jewish leaders who plotted to put Him there, but for you.

WE HAVE BEEN GIFTED WITH THE RICHES OF HIS GRACE

> *In Him we have redemption through His blood, the forgiveness of our trespasses, according to the riches of His grace 8 which He lavished on us. (Ephesians 1:7-8a).*

God could have saved us out of the riches of His grace, but He didn't. He did something better. Our salvation was "**according to** the riches of His grace."

In the 1930's, millionaire John D. Rockefeller used to dress up in a suit and a top hat and have his picture taken giving some poor boy a dime. A dime was a lot of money in those days. It would be the equivalent of $10 today. But even so, the most that could be said of Rockefeller is that he was giving out of the abundance of his riches. However, if he had gone to one of those boys and had purchased for him a mansion in the country and given him a chauffeur-driven limousine, then it could be said that he was giving according to his riches.

That is the way God has saved us. Not merely out of His riches. But according to His riches. How rich is God? How much grace does He possess? An inexhaustible supply. All of God's attributes are of infinite measure. So that if He has graced us according to the riches of His grace, then He has graced us very richly indeed.

The story is told of a missionary to Africa who had a medical condition in which he was required to drink goat's milk. He was visited one day by a tribal king and he noticed that the king was eyeing his goat. The missionary felt led of the Lord to give the goat as a gift to the king and, in return, the king presented him with the staff that he was carrying.

Later that day, the missionary confided in a friend, "I don't know what I was thinking. How could I have been so foolish as to give my goat away? I don't know what I shall do with this stick."

His friend replied, "You don't understand. That isn't a stick. It is a scepter. You don't just own one goat. Now you own all the goats in the tribe." The Lord has given us an inheritance. It is a scepter and we have been walking around thinking that it is just a stick.

WE HAVE BEEN SHOWN THE MYSTERY OF HIS WILL

> *...In all wisdom and insight* 9 *He made known to us the mystery of His will, according to His kind intention which He purposed in Him* 10 *with a view to an administration suitable to the fullness of the times, that is, the summing up of all things in Christ, things in the heavens and things on the earth. (Ephesians 1:8b-10).*

God has a plan for the universe. History is moving toward a goal. We do not have to guess at either the plan or the goal. It has been made known to us. Verse 9 says that *"He made known to us the mystery of His will."*

That was not always the case. Throughout the Old Testament era, God spoke to the fathers through the prophets, but He did not tell them everything that would come to pass in the far future. They were missing a key element of the puzzle. That has changed for us. The key element has been revealed. It is Jesus.

In the Old Testament, they knew that there was a promise of a perfect seed who would come and destroy the works of Satan. They knew of a great prophet that would come. They knew of their need for a lasting sacrifice. They knew of God's covenant promises. They knew of God's kingdom. But they did not know exactly how it would all work itself out in the plan of God. We do. The answer to the mystery is Jesus. He is the perfect seed of the woman. His death overthrew the devil and his angels. Through His blood we have entered into a greater and more perfect covenant. He is the Prophet, Priest and King. We have entered into His kingdom through faith.

We have the whole story. We have the beginning of the story in the Old Testament. We have the middle of the story in the coming of Christ, in His death, His burial, and His resurrection. We also have the end of the story, for we have His promise that one day He shall return. It will be at that time – *the fullness of the times* – that we shall experience *the summing up of all things in Christ (1:10)*. When Christ returns, the entire universe, *things in the heavens and things upon the earth*, shall be brought into conformity and into submission to Him.

What is our response to this teaching? It is that we do not have to wait until the coming of Christ to involve ourselves in such conformity. We have been called today to be both conformed and transformed into the image of Jesus Christ.

SIGNED, SEALED AND DELIVERED – THE MINISTRY OF THE SPIRIT

1. We have been Signed from eternity

> *In Him 11 also we have obtained an inheritance, having been predestined according to His purpose who works all things after the counsel of His will, 12 to the end that we who were the first to hope in Christ would be to the praise of His glory (Ephesians 1:10b-12).*

We have an inheritance. Notice the use of the present tense. We are not merely heirs of a future inheritance. It awaits us as a present possession in the heavenlies. It is an inheritance that has been awaiting us for a very long time. It has been waiting for us since before we were saved; before we were even born. We saw back in verses 4-5 that God predestined us *"before the foundation of the world."*

But there came a time when we heard the message of the gospel of salvation and we believed that message and something special happened. At that time, we entered into a covenant relationship with God. It is a new covenant, signed in the blood of Christ. And it is an everlasting covenant pointing to an everlasting relationship with Him.

2. We have been Sealed with the Spirit

> *In Him, you also, after listening to the message of truth, the gospel of your salvation – having also believed, you were sealed in Him with the Holy Spirit of promise, 14 who is given as a pledge of our inheritance (Ephesians 1:13-14a).*

We don't use seals much today. But they were commonplace throughout the ancient world. A seal would be a stamp which would be pressed into a soft surface like wax in order to leave an indelible impression. Seals served a variety of purposes.

Ancient Use	Spiritual Implication
Used on invoices to authenticate them and establish them as genuine	The Spirit's seal upon us identifies us as genuine members of God's kingdom

Indicates ownership	The Spirit's seal is an indication that we are the prized possession of God.
Ratifies a covenant or contract	Ratification of the New Covenant in Christ.
Guarantee	The Spirit is a pledge to guarantee all that we have in Christ.
Preserve and Protect (Governor's Seal placed on the tomb of Jesus)	The Spirit of God preserves and protects us from the prince of this world.

The seal of the Holy Spirit fulfills each of these purposes. It is the test of our genuine conversion. When you look at someone's life and you see the presence of the Spirit of God in that life, it is one of the evidences that such a person belongs to God. The Spirit is given as the seal of God's new covenant relationship with His people. The Lord has given a guarantee that all of His promises will be granted to us. His guarantee of His pledge is His own Spirit.

3. We have been Delivered to God as a prized package

> *...you were sealed in Him with the Holy Spirit of promise, 14 who is given as a pledge of our inheritance, with a view to the redemption of God's own possession, to the praise of His glory. (Ephesians 1:13b-14).*

You are described as God's own special possession; a trophy of His grace. You are God's, not only because He created you in the first place, but especially because He purchased you.

The story is told of a little boy who built a toy sailboat. He loved that sailboat. It held a special place in his bedroom and he would imagine sailing on exciting adventures with his toy boat. One day, he was down at the lake putting the boat in the water when the wind changed and, much to his dismay, his boat was swept away.

It was a few months later when he was walking down the street and saw the same sailboat in the window of a pawn shop. "That's my boat!" he told the pawn shop owner. "It may have been your boat," replied the owner, "but it's mine now and it will cost you twenty dollars."

The little boy went home and collected and saved until he had $20.00 and then he went back to the pawn shop and purchased the boat. "Little sailboat," he said, "You are mine. I made you and then I bought you back. You're twice mine." The Lord is our Maker. He not only made us, He also bought us and paid for us. We are twice His.

A PRAYER FOR ALL SEASONS
Ephesians 1:15-23

God has said some tremendous things about you. He has said that you are special to Him. And in this chapter, He calls you to open your eyes and see what it is that He says about you.

We have already noted that the verses 3-14 are made up in the Greek text of one very long run-on sentence. Paul begins talking about the blessings which we have in Christ Jesus and he does not stop to take a breath until the end of verse 14. Verses 15-23 form a second overly long sentence, although our English translation breaks it up into several shorter sentences.

1:1	1:3	1:15
Salutation	Blessings in Christ	
	Position and Possessions	
	Praise	**Prayer**

Verses 3-14 give Paul's praise. Now verses 15-23 give Paul's prayer. He begins His prayer with thanksgiving to the Lord. While the former section called for a blessing to *the God and Father of our Lord Jesus Christ* (1:3), now Paul prays to *the God of our Lord Jesus Christ, the Father of glory* (1:17).

A PRAYER OF THANKS

> *For this reason I too, having heard of the faith in the Lord Jesus which exists among you and your love for all the saints, 16 do not cease giving thanks for you, while making mention of you in my prayers (Ephesians 1:15-16).*

When Paul says, *"For this reason,"* he is referring back to everything he has

said up to this point. The truth that we have been...
>	Blessed
>	And chosen
>	And predestined
>	And adopted as sons
>	And redeemed
>	And forgiven
>	And given an inheritance
>	And sealed
>	And made a special possession of God...

Because of all those things, Paul gives thanks. He has heard some news about the Ephesians. It is news that drives him to his knees in thanksgiving. He has heard news that makes him believe that Christ is working in the Ephesian church.

1. He has heard of their faith in the Lord Jesus: *For this reason I too, having heard of the faith in the Lord Jesus which exists among you... (Ephesians 1:15).*

    Notice that he does not say that he has heard of *their* faith. He has heard of *the* faith which was among them. You see, Paul had already warned the Ephesians that not everyone in the church would necessarily be in the faith. He warned that there would come a time when the world would get into the church. He told the Ephesian elders that men would arise within their own church *"speaking perverse things to draw away the disciples after them" (Acts 20:30).*

    If you are a part of a local church, then there is faith among you today. But the key question is whether there is faith in you. Have you entered into the riches of the blessing of Christ Jesus? Or are you an outsider looking in? There is a litmus test given by Paul. It is your love for other Christians.

2. He has heard of their love for all the saints: *For this reason I too, having heard of the faith in the Lord Jesus which exists among you and your love for all the saints (Ephesians 1:15).*

    One of the signs of a true Christian is that he loves other true Christians. Why is that a sign? Because Christians can be rather unlovable. God didn't choose the most loveable people to be His.

God did not choose you because of any good quality that you possessed. He chose you freely and without cause.

Christians can be rather unlovable. But when you come to Christ through a heart of faith and repentance and when you recognize how much God has loved you, then your response is to begin to love other Christians.

A PRAYER FOR WISDOM AND FOR REVELATION

> *...while making mention of you in my prayers; 17 that the God of our Lord Jesus Christ, the Father of glory, may give to you a spirit of wisdom and of revelation in the knowledge of Him. (Ephesians 1:16-17).*

Having seen the evidence of their faith and their love, Paul proceeds to pray for the Ephesians. His prayer for them is that they might know something. That they might have a spirit of wisdom and of revelation in their knowledge of God.

This is the same prayer that Moses prayed for himself. In Exodus 33 God was giving a special blessing to Moses. And Moses asks of the Lord, "Show me Thy glory!" The Lord says, "You cannot see My face and continue to live, but I'll do this. I'll put you in a cleft in the rock and I'll cover you there with My hand and then I shall pass by with all of the radiance of My glory and when I have passed by, I will take My hand away and you will see My afterglow."

Paul prays the same thing for us. That as Moses saw the glory of God, that same *Father of glory* might show Himself to us. That we might be given a spirit of wisdom and of revelation in the knowledge of God - not seeing Him with physical eyes, but with the eyes of our heart.

A PRAYER FOR ENLIGHTENMENT

> *I pray that the eyes of your heart may be enlightened, so that you will know what is the hope of His calling, what*

are the riches of the glory of His inheritance in the saints, 19 and what is the surpassing greatness of His power toward us who believe. (Ephesians 1:18-19a).

Perhaps you've heard of the liturgy of knowledge.

He who...		
Thinks he knows what he does not know	is a Fool	Avoid him
Does not know that he does not know	is a Child	Teach him
Does not care that he does not know	is Lazy	Exhort him
Knows that he knows	is Wise	Follow him

Paul speaks of knowledge here. He knows that he knows and he wants you to know, too. He wants you to know three things.

I pray that the eyes of your heart may be enlightened, so that you will know...		
1:18b	1:18c	1:19
What is the hope of His calling	*What are the riches of the glory of His inheritance in the saints*	*What is the surpassing greatness of His power toward us who believe*
Position Principle: We have a position in Christ.	Possession Principle: We are the inheritance - shows that we are greatly valued.	Power Principle: This power is directed toward us who believe.
Wealth of the Christian	Worth of the Christian	Work of the Christian

1. Your Wealth: *The hope of His calling.*

    In Ephesians 2:12 Paul will talk about how there was a time when you had no hope and were without God. Hope is vital to our existence and that has never been so true as it is today.

A number of years ago, off the coast of Massachusetts, a Coast Guard cutter collided with a navy submarine. The submarine sank before anyone could escape. Ships rushed to the scene of the disaster, but there was nothing any of them could do.

Divers were sent down to evaluate the situation. The story is told how one of the divers man put his helmeted ear against the vessel and listened for any sounds. What he heard was someone tapping in Morse code. Because he knew Morse code he could decipher the message. It was this: *"Is - there - any - hope?"*

The world is asking the same thing. In this age of evolutionary philosophy when our schools and our media are proclaiming that there is no God, no meaning and no future, the world is hungry for hope.

Hope. A confident expectation. But the point here is not merely a hope in hope. The point here is that we have something in which to hope. We have a hope into which we have been called. To what have we been called? To be like Christ. To be in Him.

Because He has eternal life, we have been granted eternal life. Because He is righteous, we have been declared to be righteous by the Judge of all men. Because He is the Son of God, we have been adopted into God's forever family as His children. Because He is the Heir to the kingdom, we have become co-heirs with Christ.

God deals with us on the basis of what He sees us to be in Christ. Do you remember the story of Gideon? He was the man from Israel who was called to deliver Israel from the Midianites. A job for a real warrior. But when God first came to Gideon, he didn't look like much of a warrior. He was hiding from the very Midianites whom he was being called to fight.

Nevertheless, the angel of the Lord appeared to him and said to him, *"The Lord is with you, O Valiant Warrior."* (Judges 6:12). Why? Not because Gideon was acting in a brave manner. But because the Lord deals with us on the basis of the future. He deals with us on the basis of what He has called us to become.

He calls to an old childless couple, dry and shriveled and long past the age of bearing children, and gives the man the name of Abraham - father of a multitude. He calls to a lying trickster of a shepherd named Jacob and gives him the title of Israel, prince of God. He calls to Simon, unstable as shifting sand, and names him Peter, the rock on whom He will build His church. Then He calls you, with all of your sins and your failings and your doubts and He calls you saint, set apart as a holy vessel for the Master's special purpose.

That is not all. Our calling is not merely positional, it does not only relate to our position in Christ. It has ramifications on how I am to live today.

I have been called to be holy and now I am to live in a holy manner. I have been justified, declared to by righteous by God; now I am to live a righteous life. I am a son of God and now I am to live as befits a child of the King.

Furthermore, I have God's promise that He will bring forth the character of Christ in my life. This is the basis of my hope. It is God's work. For me. And to me. And in me.

2. Your Worth: *The riches of the glory of His inheritance in the saints.*

When we talk about riches in the Bible, we are inclined to think about the riches which God has given or will give to us. But that isn't in view here.

Look at verse 18. Do you see what are the riches? The saints! We are the riches. God has not only given you an inheritance, He has also made you to become an inheritance. You are His prized possession. Not because you are so wonderful. But because of what He is making you to become. The church. Pure and holy. His spotless bride.

Patricia McGerr tells the delightful story of Johnny Lingo, a handsome bachelor in a south Pacific village where the custom was that a man would pay a dowry to the father in order to be granted permission to marry the daughter. The average dowry price for a maiden was three cows, although an exceptionally beautiful girl might go for as high as five cows.

One day, Johnny Lingo went to the father of Sarita to negotiate a dowry. Tongues immediately began to wag, for it was well-known that Sarita was not very pretty. In fact, she was considered to be rather plain.

On the other hand, Johnny Lingo was known for being such a sharp negotiator that some speculated that he might be able to obtain Sarita for as low as one cow. However, Johnny Lingo did nothing of the sort. He marched up to Sarita's father and offered eight cows for her hand in marriage. Eight cows! It was unheard of! No one had ever paid such a high price for a bride. And for such a plain woman as Sarita!

But after the wedding, a strange thing happened. Sarita began to take on a noble bearing. Her head was held high. Her eyes sparkled. She beamed with an inner glow. And in the years that followed, she became known as the most beautiful woman in all the village. People would come from afar to see her as her radiant grace became almost legendary.

One day, Johnny Lingo was asked why he had paid such a exorbitant price for a wife. He replied, "I loved Sarita and wanted to express the high value of our marriage. Her self esteem has been greatly elevated as she realizes that her dowry price was higher than any other woman in the village." Then with a grin, he added, "But the other reason I had was that I wanted to marry an eight-cow wife."

God paid the highest possible price for you. Not merely in cows, but in His only begotten Son. And that makes you a prized possession of inestimable value.

3. Your Work: *The surpassing greatness of His power toward us who believe.*

There is now a power principle at work in my life. It is the same power that reached into a sealed tomb and made a dead man get up and walk.

> *These are in accordance with the working of the strength of His might 20 which He brought about in Christ, when He raised Him from the dead and seated Him at His right hand in the heavenly places,*

> *21 far above all rule and authority and power and dominion, and every name that is named, not only in this age but also in the one to come. (Ephesians 1:19b-21).*

When Paul wants to present the greatest of all possible manifestations of God's power, he points to the cross and specifically to the resurrection of Christ. Christ's resurrection is the forerunner of our own. He is our assurance of a future resurrection. Because He rose from the dead, we shall also rise.

That is not all. Because He rose, we have a new life now. The power that was involved in making a dead man get up and walk is the same power that is involved is saving you and in bringing about your growth as a Christian.

THE SOURCE OF ANSWERED PRAYER

> *These are in accordance with the working of the strength of His might 20 which He brought about in Christ, when He raised Him from the dead and seated Him at His right hand in the heavenly places, 21 far above all rule and authority and power and dominion, and every name that is named, not only in this age but also in the one to come. 22 And He put all things in subjection under His feet, and gave Him as head over all things to the church, 23 which is His body, the fullness of Him who fills all in all. (Ephesians 1:19b-23).*

Paul finally brings us to the source of answered prayer. It is to be found in the work of Christ on our behalf. There are four areas where that work has been manifested.

1. Resurrection: *He raised Him from the dead* (1:20).

    The resurrection of Christ is the central truth of Christianity. We believe in the One who died and who rose from the dead and who lives today. But the point here is that the same power that was involved in raising Christ from the dead is at work on your behalf. His resurrection was for you in the same way He death was for you. Because He rose from the dead, you will also rise from the dead.

Because He rose from the dead, you have new life now and it is a life that is imbued with that same resurrection power.

2. Exaltation: *Seated Him at His right hand in the heavenly places* (1:20).

Jesus has a seat of honor today. That place of honor is at the right hand of God. The right hand is the hand of honor. This was a distinction due, at least in part, to the sanitary habits of people in the ancient world. The right hand was used for eating while the left hand was used for other sanitation needs. Even today, when you travel in the Middle East, you do not shake hands with the left hand.

The right hand was the place of honor. When Jacob wanted to give the greater blessing to his younger grandson Ephraim, he crossed his hands to place his right hand upon his head (Genesis 48:17). When Solomon as the new king of Israel wished to honor his mother, he had a seat placed at his right (1 Kings 2:19). When Jesus told a parable of the sheep and the goats, it is those on His right hand who are permitted to enter the kingdom of heaven (Matthew 25:64). Psalm 110:1 describes a heavenly conversation in which David, the author of that Psalm, reports the words of the Lord:

> *The LORD says to my Lord:*
> *"Sit at My right hand*
> *Until I make Your enemies a footstool for Your feet."*

On a number of occasions, the New Testament writers report the fulfillment of these words. During His trial before the high priest, Jesus testified that *"from now on the Son of Man will be seated at the right hand of the power of God" (Luke 22:69)*. Mark 16:19 tells of how Jesus *was received up into heaven and sat down at the right hand of God*. As he was being stoned to death, Stephen reported seeing *"the heavens opened, and the Son of man standing on the right hand of God" (Acts 7:56)*.

3. Lordship: *Far above all rule and authority and power and dominion, and every name that is named, not only in this age but also in the one to come (1:21).*

The position to which Jesus has ascended is one of authority. It is not a position that will only take place at some time in the future, but one that is in effect "in this age." as well as in the one to come. There is a sense in which Jesus is reigning today. Having said that, we have to add that there is also a sense in which He is not reigning today. We have already cited the words of Psalm 110:1 where the Father says to the Son, *"Sit at My right hand until I make Your enemies a footstool for Your feet."* These words anticipate a time of waiting until all enemies are defeated. That has not yet been completed. We have not yet arrived at the day when every knee is bowing and every tongue is confessing that Jesus is Lord (Isaiah 45:23; Romans 14:11). But whether it is recognized or not, the fact remains true that Jesus is seated today in the place of all rule and authority and power and dominion.

4. Headship: *And He put all things in subjection under His feet, and gave Him as head over all things to the church, 23 which is His body, the fullness of Him who fills all in all* (1:22-23)

The capstone of the present and future authority of King Jesus to whom all things have been subjected is that He is the head of the church. This climactic statement brings the entire description of the glorified Lord into relationship with us. He is our glorified head who fills all in all. The church does not fill Christ just as Christ does not fill the Father. But the church is said to be the fullness of Christ just as Christ is said to be the fullness of the Father so that all the fullness of Deity dwells in Him in bodily form (Colossians 2:9).

The same power that accomplished all of those things is available to you. It is available for your salvation and it is available for your continued growth. You need to know this because it is impossible to live the Christian life without the power of God. Do you ever feel powerless? Like you want to obey the Lord but you just aren't up to the task? I love the prayer of second chances that goes: *"Lord, here I am - again."* Do you feel that way? Good! Because it is only when you come to the end of yourself that you are ready to experience the power of God.

"I've tried to be good and I just can't do it."
"It's impossible."
God's vocation is in the realm of the impossible. And in the same way that He raised Jesus from the dead and seated Him in the heavenlies and is going to bring all things in subjection to Him, so He shall raise you up to a new life.

Christ	Christians
Was raised from the dead	Are risen to a new life in Christ
Seated at the right hand of God	Seated with Christ in the heavenlies
Lordship in this age and in the age to come	Co-heirs with Christ
Head over the church	The body of the church

Verse 22 is the first actual mention of the church. That is us. It is in the realm of the church that Jesus is exercising His Lordship today. The church is His body on earth. It is to grow and develop as a healthy body. It is to do the work of ministry under the leadership of the head (that is what bodies do).

He has sent His church into the world to make disciples of all the nations. The result will be a called out assembly of every nation and tribe and people. That is what the church is. And your responsibility is to be the church, not just to attend one. But you can only do that as you are connected to the head - Jesus Christ.

There is a saying in the fire service that states the buildings God did not want to burn were sprinklered. Yet even in cases where the sprinklers are present, there have been problems in systems when there was an obstruction. This took place in the early 1990's at the 38-story high-rise building known as One Meridian Plaza in Philadelphia. Fire broke out on the twenty second floor and fire fighters responded and made their way up to the floor of the fire, only to find that the standpipe system was restricting the water pressure to their lines. The water was there; the standpipes were there; but the pressure relief valves had been improperly set and these caused an obstruction to the flow of water. The fire consumed eight floors and killed three fire fighters before its advance was halted by a small handful of sprinklers on the thirtieth floor.

Are you connected to Christ? Is there anything obstructing your connection to Him? He is the living water, the source of all life. His resurrection power is available to you, but only if you are connected to Him.

FROM DEATH TO LIFE
Ephesians 2:1-7

Quite a few years ago a movie was made about nostalgia and reminiscence. It was entitled, "The Way We Were." Paul begins this chapter in the same way. He begins with the way we were. But there is nothing fond or nostalgic about that former condition. There are three views concerning man and his condition before God.

View #1	"I'm okay, you're okay"	Man is basically healthy and has no serious needs outside himself.
View #2	"I'm okay, you're not so hot."	Man is sick but can improve through self effort. He needs a doctor or a coach.
View #3	We are all dead in sin"	Man is dead in his relationship to God and needs a resurrection.

It is this third view that is Biblical. It seems a very pessimistic view. It is pessimistic with regard to its view of man. But it is greatly optimistic with regard to its view of God.

When you go to a jeweler's shop and ask to look at a diamond, they will typically place the brilliant gemstone on a background of black velvet. Why do they do this? It is to allow the diamond to shine brighter. The contrast gives added perspective to the vision of the stone. In the same way, it is as we see the grace of God against the black background of our sin that we shall see the depths of beauty in God's grace.

THE WAY WE WERE

> *And you were dead in your trespasses and sins, 2 in which you formerly walked according to the course of this world, according to the prince of the power of the air, of the spirit that is now working in the sons of disobedience.*

> *Among them we too all formerly lived in the lusts of our flesh, indulging the desires of the flesh and of the mind, and were by nature children of wrath, even as the rest. (Ephesians 2:1-3).*

Paul is addressing the believers in the city of Ephesus. They had not always been believers. This city had once been a city of idol worshipers. There had been an idol-making industry there that was the basis of the city's economy. Then Christianity came to Ephesus. People's lives began to change and they began to turn from their old lifestyle.

Notice how this section begins. It is with the word "and." This takes us back to the previous chapter. These chapter divisions were not a part of the original text; they were added for our convenience. We are supposed to understand that there is a correlation of thought between chapter 1 and chapter 2. We can see this in the following chart:

Ephesians 1	**Ephesians 2**
Gives us the past, present and future of God's great plan of salvation.	Gives us the past present and future of the people whom God saves.
God's perspective.	Our perspective.
Starts with God's election prior to the creation.	Starts with our lost condition prior to salvation.
Ends with all things in subjection to Christ.	Ends with the church being built up into a dwelling of God.

In this chapter, Paul is going to focus upon God's plan of salvation from our perspective. To do this, he begins by going back to look at a time when we were lost.

The picture is not a pretty one. Indeed, it seems a rather callous thing that Paul does. How would you like someone to point out all of your past sins? Why does Paul do this? Aren't all of these past sins forgiven and forgotten? Why does Paul dredge them up?

It is because you can never fully appreciate the salvation that God has provided until you see the hopeless condition out of which you were delivered. If you ever forget where you were, then you will not be able to appreciate where you are. Grace is only great when we have seen the depths of the alternative. Light is all the more bright when you have first known the darkness.

Furthermore, Jesus said in Luke 7:47 that the one who is forgiven much will love much. There is a corollary between the greatness of your debt and your appreciation of your forgiveness. Seeing this vast gulf will cause you to love God more. This is what happens in Christianity. First you see Jesus and what He has done; then you come to love the One you have seen.

Paul describes the way we were in verses 1-3. There are four aspects to this description. We were Dead, Disobedient, Depraved and Doomed.

Dead	*And you were dead in your trespasses and sins (2:1).*
Disobedient	*You formerly walked according to the course of this world, according to the prince of the power of the air, of the spirit that is now working in the sons of disobedience (2:2).*
Depraved	*We too all formerly lived in the lusts of our flesh, indulging the desires of the flesh and of the mind... (2:3)*
Doomed	*And were by nature children of wrath (2:3).*

1. We were Dead: *And you were dead in your trespasses and sins (Ephesians 2:1).*

    This is speaking of spiritual death. Notice that death does not indicate inactivity, but separation. You may have been very active in your spiritual death – most unbelievers are. But you were spiritually dead. There was nothing in you that was connected to God.

    > Some translations place the subject and predicate of the sentence, "God" and "made alive" in verse 1 and then repeat them in their proper location of verse 4-5. But this fails to show the emphasis of total hopelessness which this passage teaches we have without Christ.

    Too many times we think of unbelievers as being spiritually sick.

Give them a "spiritual pill" and they'll get better. But the Biblical picture of man's condition is much worse than that. He is dead. He doesn't need a teacher. Or a guide. Or a doctor. He needs a miracle. He needs a resurrection.

People read this and have trouble identifying with it. This should come as no surprise, for a corpse does not know it is dead. A corpse does not respond to outside stimuli. It is not until you breathe new life into a corpse that it can respond. A corpse does not need motivation or teaching or assistance. A corpse needs a resurrection.

> Telling an unbeliever to clean up his life is like telling a dead man in a grave to clean up his coffin.

In the last chapter we read of the power that raised up Christ from the dead. Now we see the importance of that power – it was necessary because you were spiritually dead. The same power that raised up Christ from physical death was necessary to raise you up from spiritual death.

2. **We were Disobedient:** *In which you formerly walked according to the course of this world, according to the prince of the power of the air, of the spirit that is now working in the sons of disobedience (Ephesians 2:2).*

We saw in verse 1 that we were described as dead. Here in verse 2 we see that we were among the walking dead. We were zombies and we walked in a set path. It was not in the path of obedience toward God. Our path was in accordance to that which is set against God. Our path was in accordance to two courses.

> Note that the course of the walk is a symptom of being spiritually dead.

a. We walked in the way of the world.

The world is in rebellion toward God. It is in sin. And it suffers the natural result of sin. Have you ever noticed what it is that your kids tell you when you tell them that they can't do something. "But everyone else is doing it!" They are appealing to the course of this world. It is an appeal to a sinful standard.

    b.   We walked in the way of the devil.

        He is not called the devil in this passage (he will be so identified in Ephesians 6:11). Instead, we see him described with two other titles.

        (1)   The prince of the power of the air.

            Satan is elsewhere called *"the prince of this world"* (John 12:31; 14:30; 16:11) and was described by the Jews as the *"prince of demons"* (Matthew 9:34; 12:24).

            In both Jewish and Greek thought, the air was viewed as the abode of the demons. These demons were unseen powers (see the use of the term *"powers"* in Ephesians 6:12).

            There is a point here. It is that the forces of Satan are not "down there" but rather "up here." Satan is not far away and long ago. He is in the nasty here and now. We shall come back to this subject in Ephesians 6 when we speak of the spiritual warfare in which we are combatants.

        (2)   The spirit that is now working in the sons of disobedience.

            Satan's activity is not merely in the past. He is still working. His work is seen in every disobedient act.

3.   We were Depraved: *Among them we too all formerly lived in the lusts of our flesh, indulging the desires of the flesh and of the mind... (Ephesians 2:3a).*

Up to this point, Paul has been speaking in the 2nd person plural – all of you. Paul is speaking to the church at Ephesus. They are predominantly Gentiles. But now there is a change. Now he switches to the 1st person plural – we.

Gentiles	**Jews and Gentiles**
2:1 **YOU** *were dead in your trespasses and sins in which you formerly walked*	2:3 **WE ALL** *formerly lived in the lusts of our flesh*
according to the course of this world *according to the prince* *of the power of the air* *of the spirit that is now working in the sons of disobedience*	*indulging the desires* *of the flesh* *and* *of the mind,* *and* *were by nature children of wrath even as the rest*

If verses 1-2 relate specifically to those who were raised as pagans, verse 3 relates to those who had a religious upbringing. They were no less in need of a Savior. Indeed, the fact that both groups were dead in their sins will be reiterated in verse 5: *"even when **we** were dead in our transgressions..."*

Notice the reference to living in the lusts of the flesh. The Greek turn translated lust is ἐπιθυμια (*epithumia*). It describes a passion. Depending upon the context, it can be a good passion or a bad passion. Jesus uses this term in Luke 22:15 when He speaks of how He **earnestly** longed to eat the Passover with His disciples. It is not evil to be passionate, but this is speaking of a fleshly, indulgent passion. It is a passion centered upon self instead of upon God.

4. We Were Doomed: *And were by nature children of wrath, even as the rest. (Ephesians 2:3b).*

Instead of being children of God, we were *"children of wrath."* We were on a road to judgment and we were following the one whose destiny was eternal judgment. This is what we were *by nature*.

The reason that unbelievers act like unbelievers is that they are unbelievers by their very nature. It does not matter if they are religious. They are just as lost as the most lost pagan. It is their nature.

This is why it is useless to talk about reform without regeneration. It is like taking a pig and washing him and dousing him with perfume and dressing him up in a suit and a tie and putting little shoes on his feet and giving him lessons in etiquette. Let him alone near the slop pile and you will see him acting the part of a pig. Why? Because he has a piggy nature.

You need a new nature. You need that old person who was by nature a child of wrath to be crucified, dead and buried and you need to be reborn and resurrected as a child of the King. And that is exactly what God has brought about in Christ.

A RADICAL REMEDY

> *But God, being rich in mercy, because of His great love with which He loved us, 5 even when we were dead in our transgressions, made us alive together with Christ (by grace you have been saved), 6 and raised us up with Him, and seated us with Him in the heavenly places in Christ Jesus, 7 so that in the ages to come He might show the surpassing riches of His grace in kindness toward us in Christ Jesus. (Ephesians 2:4-7).*

A chess master was walking through an art museum when he came upon a painting entitled, "Checkmate." It depicted a cowering man playing a game of chess against a looming figure who represented Satan. The master stopped and gazed for a long time at the painting, noting the terror of the man and the smug satisfaction of his opponent. Then his gaze moved down to the chessboard and he examined the artist's rendition of the pieces on the board. Suddenly, the master cried out, "Wait, there is one more move!"

> Verses 4-7 consists of a single sentence. Paul is going to tell you what you did when you came to Christ, but before he does, he first wants to tell you...
> - What God is like: Rich in mercy.
> - Why God did what He did: Because of His great love.
> - The depths from which God saved us.

So it is with us. In the first three verses of this chapter, God shows us the hopelessness of our former condition. We were dead, disobedient, depraved and doomed. But then the Master points out that there is still one more move.

It is one that makes all the difference in the world.

This section is introduced with the conjunction, "but." We were dead, but God made us alive. We were disobedient in following after the world and the devil, but God raised us out of the world and out of the domain of the devil. We were depraved, but God seated us with Christ and gave us a new nature. We were doomed, but God showed us the surpassing riches of His grace.

	The Way We Were		What God Did
Y O U	Were dead in your trespasses and sins	**B U T G O D**	Made us alive together with Christ
	Walked... according to the course of this world according to the prince / the spirit		Raised us up with Him
	Formerly lived in the lust of our flesh		Seated us with Him

With this simple conjunction ($\delta\epsilon$), we are transported from death to life, from the darkness of the grave to the light of everlasting life.

1.   Your Salvation is caused by God's Love.

> *But God, being rich in mercy, because of His great love with which He loved us(Ephesians 2:4).*

God saved us because He loved us. His love is the motivation for His being rich in mercy toward us. What is mercy? It speaks to the compassion of God. It is the quality that looks at a desperate need and then moves to fill that need. There is a fine shade of meaning between the concepts of God's mercy and God's grace.

Grace	Mercy
Unmerited favor	Compassion
Focus upon the need of man	Focus upon the misery of man

God is rich in mercy. His mercy is everlasting. That is good, having seen the depth of our misery. Gordon Clark points out that the defectiveness of the Arminian view of the greatness of God's love:

> Since for them Christ's death does not necessitate the salvation of any particular person, God can only love mankind in general. Christ did not die for me; he died only for an unidentified group of people who would happen to be wise enough to exercise faith later on. But it is hard to speak of love's being directed to no one in particular. No doubt some liberal politicians have or profess to have sympathy for the poor; but can Jim Blunt of Arkanabama speak of the great love with which Senator Ted Kennedy loved me? (1985:66).

The point is well made. It is true that God so loved the world in the general sense. But that love also became personal. He loved us and then He acted on our behalf.

2. Your Salvation is for Life.

> *Even when we were dead in our transgressions, made us alive together with Christ (Ephesians 2:5a).*

By saying that your salvation is for life, I do not mean that your salvation is forever. It is that. But that is not what I mean by this statement. I mean that your salvation is for the purpose of life. You have been saved so that you can be alive. God has made you alive together with Christ. Christ has given you a new life. You no longer have to merely exist, you can now really live.

You have died, been buried and have been resurrected from the dead. You might say, "My body doesn't show it." That is because your body hasn't caught up with you, yet. But it will one day.

3. Your Salvation is by Grace.

> *...even when we were dead in our transgressions, made us alive together with Christ (by*

grace you have been saved)... (Ephesians 2:5).

The parentheses at the end of verse 5 is an important one. It tells us that your salvation is on the basis of grace. Grace is the unmerited and undeserved favor of God. That means you don't deserve to be saved. You can't earn it and you can't deserve it.

You aren't saved because you aren't guilty. You are saved in spite of the fact that you are guilty. We shall have more to say about this when we get to verse 8.

4. Your Salvation is Complete.

> *And raised us up with Him, and seated us with Him in the heavenly places in Christ Jesus (Ephesians 2:6).*

What does it mean to be seated? It means that the work is finished. That the victory is complete. When a priest went into the temple, the one thing that he never did was to sit down. He was always standing in the presence of God. Even when the animal sacrifice had been offered, he still stood. Because the next day there would have to be another sacrifice offered. And another. And another. It was never-ending. But Jesus was the final sacrifice. When He died upon the cross, He said, "It is finished!"

Because Jesus has completed the work of our salvation, He has sat down at the right hand of the Father. If we are united with Him through faith, we have a new identity. The person we have become in Him is now qualified to enter into the presence of God. We are considered to be seated with Him in heaven.

5. Your Salvation has a Purpose.

> *So that in the ages to come He might show the surpassing riches of His grace in kindness toward us in Christ Jesus. (Ephesians 2:7).*

The purpose of your salvation is everlasting. It is so that throughout eternity you might be a trophy of God's grace and His kindness in Christ. You will be the display of what God has done to deliver a human life from the bondage of sin.

In the second year of the War Between the States, an informer in the prison camp at Palmyra disappeared. The Commander in charge ordered that ten men would be shot in reprisal. One of those men was William T. Humphrey, a husband and father of a number of children.

Hearing that Humphrey was under the sentence of death, a young man named Hiram Smith came forward, explaining that he was unmarried and without a family. He asked permission to take the place of Humphrey, stating that perhaps it would be better for a single man to die than a man with a family.

If you go to the cemetery of the Mount Pleasant Church in what used to be the town of Mount Salem, you will find a stone that has been erected with the following inscription:

> *"This monument is dedicated to the memory of Hiram Smith. The hero who sleeps beneath the sod here was shot in Palmyra, October 17, 1862 as a substitute for William T. Humphrey, my father."*

That is what Christ has done for us. He has become our substitute. As a result, we have become an eternal monument to the riches of His mercy and to the overabundance of His grace.

FAITH & WORKS
Ephesians 2:8-10

I am the master of my fate;
I am the captain of my soul.

So go the words of W. E. Henley in his well-known Invictus. There is something intensely individualistic and ego-affirming in the idea that you make your own way. We would all like to think that we can pull ourselves up by our own bootstraps. We like the idea of being in charge of our lives. The problem is that it is not entirely true.

There is an old story that tells of a man who was traveling on his donkey when he came upon a small fuzzy object lying in the road. He dismounted to look more closely and found a sparrow lying on its back with its scrawny legs thrust upward. At first he thought the bird was dead, but closer investigation proved it to be very much alive. The man asked the sparrow if he was all right. The sparrow replied, "Yes." The man asked, "What are you doing lying on your back with your legs pointed towards the sky?" The sparrow responded that he had heard a rumor that the sky was falling, and so he was holding his legs up to catch it. The man retorted, "You surely don't think that you're going to hold it up with those two scrawny legs, do you?" The sparrow, with a very solemn look, replied, "One does the best he can."

Our problem is like the problem of the sparrow. We might try to do the best we can, but our best is not good enough. Indeed, our most noble efforts seem altogether puny compared with what is really needed. When the sky is falling, our reaction might be to lift our hands to stop it, but it will do us no good.

The issue here is not the falling of the sky, but the falling of God's judgment. Man's natural response is not to lift his arms or his legs, but to act as the captain of his soul and to take charge of his fate, overcoming that judgment by depending upon his own works to save himself. Such a course is doomed to failure. This passage teaches that salvation is an act of God's free grace.

THE MEANS OF YOUR SALVATION

For by grace you have been saved through faith; and that not of yourselves, it is the gift of God; 9 not as a result of works, so that no one may boast. (Ephesians 2:8-9).

This passage contrasts both how we have been saved and how we have not been saved.

How You Have Been Saved	How You Have Not Been Saved
You have been saved by grace through faith	*You have not been saved of yourselves*
It is the gift of God	*It is not as a result of works*

There are only two possible ways to be saved. The first is through the effort of another. The second is through self effort. I once saw Dr. James Kennedy, the original founder and chancellor of Knox Theological Seminary, demonstrate these two ways in a graphic portrayal. To illustrate the first way of salvation, he turned and pointed to the cross at the front of the sanctuary. To illustrate the second way of salvation, he turned away from the cross and pointed to himself.

Paul does the same thing in this verse. He mentions the positive first. He then further explains it by contrasting it with the negative.

1. Grace: The Basis of your Salvation.

    Verse 8 says, *"For by grace you have been saved..."* The word "grace" is translated from the Greek word *charis* (χαρις). It is related to the word *charisma* (χαρισμα) – "gift," from which we get our modern word "charismatic." Grace describes that which is freely given. It is not earned or deserved. It is a gift.

    While this is related to mercy, I believe it to be more than mercy. Mercy is when you are pulled over by a policeman for doing 50 miles per hour in a zone where the speed limit is 30 and he does not give you a ticket.

Grace is when that same policeman not only refrains from giving you a ticket but also invites you over to his house for dinner.

You have been saved by grace. You do not deserve to be saved. You cannot earn this salvation. It is a free gift. When you try to pay for it, you negate the very concept of a gift, for a gift, by its very nature, is something for which the recipient did not pay.

2. The Fact of your Salvation.

    The verb "you have been saved" is a perfect passive indicative. The perfect tense points back to an action that took place in the past, but which had continuing results. You were saved in the past with the result that you are still saved.

    This tense takes us back to the actions of God in verses 4-7. God made us alive. And raised us up with Christ. And seated us with Him. And the point of this tense is that we are still alive and still raised up and still seated with Him.

    The passive voice means that salvation was something which was done to you. You did not save yourself. You were not able to save yourself. You needed a savior.

    A dead man cannot raise himself up. He needs someone to do it for him. You needed a miracle. And God provided that miracle on your behalf.

    The indicative mood is the mood of reality. It means that it really happened. When you awaken in the middle of the night and ask, "Is it really true?" be assured that God has spoken and has given His word with regard to your salvation. You can trust Him.

3. Faith: The Instrument of your Salvation.

    Before we speak of what faith is, let me pause for a moment to say what faith is not.

    - Faith is not mere knowledge.
      James 2:19 says that *"the devils believe and tremble"* - they have faith that God exists, but this is not the same as saving faith.

- Faith is not a mere subjective feeling. True faith has content. It is based upon objective facts.

- Faith is not optimism or a positive mental attitude. Motivational speakers like to talk about how you need to have faith in yourself. But having faith in yourself only works if there is something in yourself that is worthy of that faith.

There are three elements in faith.

a. The first element of faith is knowledge.

Faith must have some root in fact or else it is mere wistful thinking. There must be some objective fact which is to be believed.

Our faith is not in faith. There is an object to our faith. The object of our faith is Jesus Christ. We believe that He died for us and that He was buried and that He rose again. We believe that His death, burial, and resurrection had a result of purchasing our salvation.

b. The second element of faith is appropriation.

Knowing that Christ died is a mere knowledge of a historical event. Salvation requires knowing that He died for ME. I must appropriate that sacrifice that He made and see that it was on my own behalf.

c. The third element of faith is commitment.

This is where I accept Him as my Lord and Savior. It involves casting myself upon Christ, resting on His promises, and joining His forever family.

Jean Francois Gravalet was the most famous acrobat of the 1800's. Known as the Great Blondin, he became famous for crossing Niagara Falls on a tightrope 1,100 feet long and 160 feet above the water. Before an amazed crowd, he pushed a wheelbarrow across while blindfolded. Then he went back out and stood on his head on the wire. Finally, he carried a man across Niagara Falls on his back. When he had put the rider down, he looked into the crowd and asked a man standing near, "Do you believe I could do that with you?"

"Of course," the man answered, "I've just seen you do it." Then Blondin said, "Hop on, I'll carry you across." The man called back, "Not on your life!"

The man wouldn't go across with Blondin because he didn't really believe. He had intellectual understanding. But he didn't have real faith because he neither appropriated nor committed himself. He believed that Blondin could do it, but he wasn't willing to stake his life on it.

True faith in Jesus means that we stake our lives on Him. We commit ourselves to Him as our only hope for salvation. We give ourselves totally to Him, and burn our bridges behind us.

These three aspects to faith (knowledge, appropriation and commitment) are akin to a marriage relationship.

Faith	Marriage
Knowledge	Courtship
Appropriation	"Will you marry me?"
Commitment	The Wedding

4. The Gift of your Salvation: *It is the gift of God (Ephesians 2:8)*.

We have already noted that the words "grace" (*charis*) and "gift" (*charisma*) are related. But here we have a different word for "gift." This word is *doron* (δωρον). This word focuses upon the fact that the gift has been given (from διδωμι, "to give").

Charis – Χαρις	*Doron* – Δωρον
Focus upon the graciousness of the gift.	Focus upon the giving of the gift.

You have been given a gift. It is not merely a loan. When you are given a loan, repayment is expected, but a gift does not anticipate repayment.

5. Not as a result of Works: *Not as a result of works (Ephesians 2:9).*

   You cannot work for a gift. If you work for it, then it is wages earned. When your boss gives you a paycheck, you do not accept it and say, "Thank you for this wonderful gift!" You worked for it. You earned it. It is your just wage.

   The Bible teaches that you have a just wage. There is something for which you have worked and which you deserve. It is death.

   > *For the wages of sin is death, but the free gift of God is eternal life in Christ Jesus our Lord. (Romans 6:23).*

   People sometime ask why a loving God would send people to hell, but the question itself makes an unfounded premise. It assumes that God is doing the sending when people go to hell. The truth is that people work their way to hell. Death is the ultimate paycheck.

6. Boasting is excluded: *Not as a result of works, so that no one may boast. (Ephesians 2:9).*

   You cannot boast in your salvation. You cannot even boast in your faith. Boasting in your faith would be like boasting in the fact that you reached out to take a check from somebody. Suppose you have a tremendous debt but someone offers to pay it for you, writes out a check for you for $500,000. And you reach out and take it from him. How absurd it would be if you then went around saying to everybody, "Isn't it wonderful that I had what it took to reach out and grab that check?" The wonderful thing would not be that you had received the gift, but that it was given in the first place.

   One Sunday, the pastor of a church in London saw a former burglar kneeling beside a judge of the Court of England – the very judge who had sent him to jail where he had served seven years. After his release this burglar had been converted and become a Christian worker. Yet, as they knelt there, the judge and the former convict, neither one seemed to be aware of the other.

After the service, the judge was walking out with the pastor and the former said to him, "Did you notice who was kneeling beside me at the Communion rail this morning?" The pastor replied, "Yes, but I didn't know that you noticed." The two walked along in silence for a few moments, and then the judge exclaimed, "What a miracle of grace!" The pastor nodded in agreement. "Yes, what a marvelous miracle of grace." Then the judge said, "But to whom do you refer?" And the pastor replied, "Why, to the conversion of that convict."

The judge said, "But I was not referring to him. I was thinking of myself." The pastor, surprised, replied: "You were thinking of yourself? I don't understand."

"Yes," the judge replied, "It was natural for the burglar to receive God's grace when he came out of jail. He had nothing but a history of crime behind him, and when he saw Jesus as his Savior he knew there was salvation and hope and joy for him. He knew how much he needed that help. But look at me. I was taught from earliest infancy to live as a gentleman; that my word was to be my bond; that I was to say my prayers, go to church, take Communion, and so on. I went through Oxford, took my degrees, was called to the bar and eventually became a judge. Pastor, it was God's grace that drew me; it was God's grace that opened my heart to receive it. I'm a greater miracle of his grace."

If salvation had been the result of our own merit, our own intellect, our own efforts, or even our own decision-making ability, we would have something about which to boast. However, salvation is by grace through faith. It is a gift that I can only accept and that excludes all boasting.

THE PURPOSE OF YOUR SALVATION

For we are His workmanship, created in Christ Jesus for good works, which God prepared beforehand so that we would walk in them. (Ephesians 2:10).

In verse 9 we saw that salvation does not come on the basis of works. Here we read that salvation does not come apart from works. We are not saved by

> "We are saved by faith alone, but not by faith that is alone." - Martin Luther.

works; but we are saved for works. It is our new life purpose for which we were saved. This idea is introduced by juxtaposition of the terms for works and workmanship.

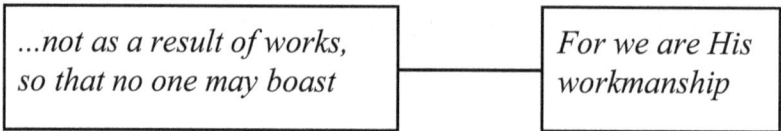

This is presented by way of a contrast. Our salvation is not as a result of our own works. The reason this is so is that we are the result of His workmanship.

1. Workmanship versus Work.

    It needs to be noted that the Greek word for "workmanship" is not related to the word for "works" which is used in verses 9 and 10.

    "Works" in verse 9 is translated from *ergon* (ἐργων). The term "workmanship" in verse 10 is *poima* (ποιμα). It comes from the simple root word *poeio* (ποιεω) which describes "doing" something. The "ma" (μα) ending gives it the added idea of a result. The only other place where this word with this specific ending is found is in Romans 1:20 where it describes the "things which are made." Thus, this passage tells us that we are "the result of God's doing."

    Think about this. In the same way that God has made the universe and it exists as the result of "His making," so also we exist as Christians who are created unto good works as the direct result of "His making."

2. His Workmanship.

    > An artist is known by the quality of his workmanship. If we are His workmanship, how should we live? Do you portray yourself as a Picaso or as an inkblot?

    When we think of the workmanship of God, we normally think of the wonders of the universe. The expanse of the galaxies. The wonders of the sun and the moon and the stars. Or perhaps we might think of the inner universe and how we are fearfully and wonderfully made and how each strand of our DNA contains more information than the most complex computer.

These are indeed wonderful. But what is more wonderful still is that God is making the very character of Christ in us.

> *For we are His workmanship, created in Christ Jesus for good works... (Ephesians 2:10a).*

Paul talks about what we are and why we are. Our identity is seen in the phrase, *His workmanship*. Our purpose is seen in the phrase, *for good works*.

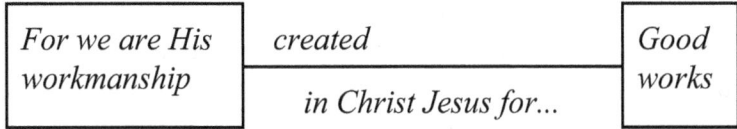

But that is not all. God has not only prepared us for good works when He made us His workmanship, He has also prepared good works for us.

3. The Sovereignty of God's Work.

The works which you have been called to work have been preordained and pre-prepared by God. Not only was your salvation predestined by God (we saw that in chapter 1), but also your good works were predestined by God.

Why does Paul tell us this? It is for our encouragement. It means that we can relax and know that God has planned the course of our Christian service. It means that we can trust Him for His leading.

> We do not keep our salvation through these works. But we do reveal our salvation by doing what saved people do – good works.

A HOUSE UNITED
Ephesians 2:11-22

A number of years ago, I received a package from Germany. Getting packages from Germany is no novelty, as my older brother has been a missionary pastor there for many years and this particular package indicated that it had been sent by him. When I opened it up, it was to find a bit of odd-colored crumbling masonry, speckled with reds and blues. I looked at it for a moment, wondering if he had attempted to ship a pot and whether the mail handlers had been particularly brutal. Then I remembered what had happened only weeks earlier in Germany. The Berlin wall had come down. A city which had been divided for nearly forty years was reunited. It turned out that my brother had been in the city of Berlin as they were tearing down the wall and had taken a bit of the masonry as a memento of the event.

If you had traveled to Jerusalem in the days of the Apostle Paul, you would have found another wall. It wasn't lined with machine-gun turrets or barbed wire. But it was no less divisive. It was a rather low stone wall, only about three or four feet high. It surrounded the Temple. It divided the outer court of the Temple, known as the Court of the Gentiles, from the inner court. A number of gates were placed into this wall at strategic locations. And by each gate, there was posted a sign. The sign held a warning in three languages: Hebrew, Greek and Latin. It warned that no Gentile was permitted past this point on pain of death.

You see, the Gentiles were excluded from worshiping God in the temple. They could come and worship from afar. But they were excluded from the community of God's people. They were outsiders. It was death for them to come closer.

Indeed, as Paul writes to the Ephesians from a Roman prison, the reason for his initial arrest was because of a riot that had taken place when it was thought that he had brought a Gentile past the wall.

Paul had a ministry to the Gentiles. He was noted as the apostle to the Gentiles. There were a number of Gentiles who labored with him in the ministry.

Paul had not always been like this. He had started out as a racist. His racism extended back all the way to his father and to his father's father – back all the way to Abraham. He had a cultural heritage of racism, of holding himself separate and aloof from all Gentiles. That all changed when he came to Christ.

THE WAY WE WERE

> *Therefore remember that formerly you, the Gentiles in the flesh, who are called "Uncircumcision" by the so-called "Circumcision," which is performed in the flesh by human hands -- 12 remember that you were at that time separate from Christ, excluded from the commonwealth of Israel, and strangers to the covenants of promise, having no hope and without God in the world. (Ephesians 2:11-12).*

Paul is writing to believers in the city of Ephesus. They are mostly Gentiles. They are known as being the *"Uncircumcision."* They are described in such a manner by "the so-called circumcision." Paul describes this as the circumcision that is *performed in the flesh by human hands*. While this is a factual description, it is couched in words that deliberately contain a negative connotation. When you read in the Old Testament of that which was made by human hands, the thing that normally comes to mind is the making of an idol. This identical phrasing regularly refers in the Septuagint to idols that were made with human hands (Leviticus 26:1; 26:30; Isaiah 2:18; 10:11; 19:1; 21:9; 31:7; 46:6; Daniel 5:4; 5:23). The truth is that the Jews had taken their circumcision and had made an idol of the practice.

By contrast, the Gentiles to whom Paul writes do not share in their bodies the sign of the Abrahamic covenant. They had been real idol worshipers.

They were....	
Separate	from Christ
Shut off	from the commonwealth of Israel
Strangers	to the covenant of promise

The Jews had the promise of a Messiah. They were the commonwealth of

Israel, God's holy nation. They were bound to God through his covenant promises. The Gentiles had none of these.

As we hear of Paul talking about how we used to be, we are reminded of a similar passage earlier in this chapter. The general outline is the same. First Paul speaks of their former condition in sin. Then he describes what God has done in bringing salvation.

Ephesians 2:1-10	Ephesians 2:11-22
You were dead in your trespasses and sins (2:1).	You were at that time separate from Christ (2:12).
You formerly lived in the lusts of your flesh (2:3).	Excluded from the commonwealth of Israel (2:12).
Indulging the desires of the flesh and of the mind (2:3).	Strangers to the covenants of promise (2:12).
And were by nature children of wrath (2:3)	Having no hope and without God in the world (2:12).
But God made us alive together with Christ (2:4-5).	But you have been brought near by the blood of Christ (2:13).

Paul says that they were *"without God."* The Greek says that they were *atheoi* (ἄθεοι) – atheists. How about you? Are you an atheist? You might reply, "Of course not! I believe in a Supreme Being, someone who is bigger than I am." But are you living your life as though there was no God? If you are not loving Him with all of your heart and all of your soul and all of your body and if you are not serving him, then you are a practicing atheist.

WHAT GOD HAS DONE – PEACE

But now in Christ Jesus you who formerly were far off have been brought near by the blood of Christ.
For He Himself is our peace, who made both groups into one and broke down the barrier of the dividing wall, 15 by abolishing in His flesh the enmity, which is the Law of commandments contained in ordinances, so that in Himself He might make the two into one new man, thus establishing

peace, 16 and might reconcile them both in one body to God through the cross, by it having put to death the enmity.

And He came and preached peace to you who were far away, and peace to those who were near; 18 for through Him we both have our access in one Spirit to the Father. (Ephesians 2:13-18).

Just when things are seen to be as bad as they can get, we are introduced to a conjunction of contrast. Here is how things were... But now things are different. You were formerly far off... But now you have been brought near.

Notice the change in the time and in the kind of action. The movement is from the continuous linear action to focus on a certain point in time.

Verse	Greek Tense	Time of Action	Kind of Action
2:11-12	Imperfect	Past	Continuous
2:13	Aorist	Past	Point of time

We were continually separated from Christ and shut off from Israel and strangers to the covenant. But then something happened in a point of time. That something is Jesus. He did a work that brought us near to God. John Stott points out that this reference to drawing near had distinctly Jewish connotations:

> Such spatial language ('far' and 'near') was not uncommon in the Old Testament. God and Israel were known to be 'near' one another, since God had promised to be their God and to make them his people. Hence Moses could say: 'What great nation is there that has a God so near to it as the Lord our God is to us?' (1979:97).

The means of your drawing near was not as a result of your own self effort. It was "not of works" (2:9). Rather, it was through the blood of Christ. When we talk of blood, we are talking covenant language. When you made a covenant in the ancient world, you would seal it through a sacrifice. You would seal it in blood. Indeed, one did not sign a covenant. You would **cut** a covenant. The old way of making a covenant was to kill an animal and cut it into two parts. The parties would walk between these parts to signify the bond as if to say that either party breaking this bond would similarly be killed. This is the significance of the blood of Christ. The covenant into which we have entered was signed in His blood. He is both the maker of the covenant as well as the substance of the covenant. When He went to the cross, He was being judged as though He had been a covenant breaker, taking upon Himself the judgment we deserved for breaking the covenant.

Verses 13-18 are presented in the form of a chiasm. Notice the alternate uses of the words "peace" and "enmity." They form a pattern that takes us through the passage.

> But now in Christ Jesus you who formerly were far off have been **brought near** by the blood of Christ. (2:13).
>> He Himself is our **peace**, who made both groups into one and broke down the barrier (2:14).
>>> Abolishing in His flesh the **enmity** (2:15).
>>>> so that in Himself He might make the two into **one new man** (2:15).
>>>>> thus establishing **peace** (2:15)
>>>> and might reconcile them both in **one body** to God through the cross (2:16).
>>> Having put to death the **enmity** (2:16).
>> He came and preached **peace** to you who were far away and **peace** to those who were near (2:17).
> For through Him we both have our **access** in one Spirit to the Father (2:18).

The way in which Jesus brought about peace involved the destruction of those things which stood in the way of peace. Notice the destructive ministry of Jesus as it is described here.

Verse	Greek Word	Translation
2:14	Lusas (λυσας)	***Broke down** (literally, "destroyed") the barrier of the dividing wall*

2:15	Katargesas (καταργησας)	***Abolishing*** *in His flesh the enmity*
2:16	Apokteinas (ἀποκτειναϛ)	*Having **put to death** the enmity*

There had been no greater enmity than that which existed between Jews and Gentiles. The Jews called the Gentiles "dogs" (even Jesus made reference to them in this way in Mark 7 and if this gives you problems, then see my commentary on the Gospel of Mark).

> God did not call Israel to be a reservoir, but rather to be a channel of His blessings to the world. The church also runs the risk of becoming an elitist country club instead of reaching out to the world with the gospel.

- It was said among the Jews that Gentiles were created by God as fuel for hell.

- The Jews believed that Israel was the only nation loved by God and that all others were hated by Him.

- When a Jew returned to his homeland, he would pause at the border and shake off the Gentile dust from his clothing.

- If a Jewish boy or girl married a Gentile, the Jewish family would hold a funeral, indicating that the one who had done this was considered dead to the family.

Neither were Gentiles above persecuting the Jews. Antisemitism was not a new phenomenon. There had once been an attempt in the days of Xerxes, king of Persia, to pass an ordinance to exterminate the Jewish race; the story of that attempted genocide is related in the book of Esther. On another occasion, Jews had been forbidden to read their own Scriptures or to circumcise their young on pain of death. In Paul's day, all Jews had been banished from the city of Rome.

There was hatred between Jews and Gentiles that went in both directions with Jews hating Gentiles and with Gentiles hating Jews. Hatred is a powerful concept. But that is exactly the concept that is described in the term "enmity." There was an enmity that separated us from God. It was our hatred of God and His hatred of our sin. That enmity was put to death on the cross. Our hate met the love of Christ and it died.

This has great application for the church today. It means that the church has a basis for racial reconciliation. Between Jew and Gentile. Between Black and White. Between Anglo and Hispanic. We worship the Prince of Peace and we are to be people of peace.

The curse of Babel was visually overturned at Pentecost. The barrier of those languages that had once served to divide people of differing races was crossed in a miraculous work of the Holy Spirit. The implication of that event is that our racial distinctions should no longer divide us.

WHAT GOD IS DOING – A BUILDING

So then you are no longer strangers and aliens, but you are fellow citizens with the saints, and are of God's household, 20 having been built on the foundation of the apostles and prophets, Christ Jesus Himself being the corner stone, 21 in whom the whole building, being fitted together, is growing into a holy temple in the Lord, 22 in whom you also are being built together into a dwelling of God in the Spirit. (Ephesians 2:19-22).

God has a continuing work in the church today. It is a work of unification. Three illustrations are given in verses 19-20 to picture the unification of Jews and Gentiles.

A City	*Fellow citizens with the saints*
A Family	*Of God's household*
A Building	*Having been built* (the building is actually a Temple)

God is building a house. Its foundation is upon the apostles and prophets. Christ is the cornerstone. This brings us to a question. Why are the apostles and prophets called the foundation of the house? Why is Christ pictured as the cornerstone? Why isn't He the foundation?

It is the apostles and prophets who presented the truth of the work of Christ to men who believed and became a part of the building. The Ephesians had never met Jesus in the flesh. But they did meet Paul and Silas. They laid the foundation of their faith.

Christ is the cornerstone. The cornerstone holds the two adjoining walls together. Christ holds the Jews and the Gentiles together. If you are in Christ, then you are a part of that building. You have been fitted together with me and with the rest of the church. We are a building. And not just a building, but a temple. You know what a temple is. It is a place where you go to meet God. It is a place where God abides.

We are the temple. This is not speaking of us individually. We are individually temples of God and that truth is seen in 1 Corinthians 6:19, but that is not what Paul is talking about here.

> Being in Christ is never an individualistic concept. When someone does not want to be a part of a fellowship of Christians, he is being independent. The principle of Christianity is interdependence.

This is not speaking of us as individuals. This is speaking of the collective of the church. All of God's people make up this single temple.

Think of it! Those who at one time made it their practice to worship false gods and goddesses in the heathen temples of Ephesus were brought into the commonwealth of God's covenant community to become a part of the very temple of God on earth. Whereas there was a time when Gentiles were forbidden to come into the temple in Jerusalem, now we find that Gentiles have become an integral part of God's spiritual temple.

This is a marvelous thing that God has done. He has made a single body of diverse peoples. Not two bodies. Not an Old Testament Israel and a New Testament Church. One body. One temple. To serve as the dwelling place for One Spirit.

My older brother was in Berlin in the early 1990's when they tore down the dividing wall. It was to him a moving experience to stand on the site of the old wall and share the gospel of freedom with a guard in that location where they used to shoot people who attempted to escape the tyranny of communism.

I still have in my study a crumbling bit of masonry that once was a part of that Berlin Wall. I keep it as a reminder that the gospel breaks down walls. It also unites people and it also builds up a house where God dwells.

THE MYSTERY OF CHRIST
Ephesians 3:1-13

Everyone loves a mystery. There is something compelling about a search for the unknown, the bringing to light of that which has been previously hidden. I love the little boy in the movie, *A Christmas Story* where he digs through the box of Cracker Jacks to find the "Secret Decoder Ring." There is something of that little boy in all of us who itch to hear about that which has been secret.

Throughout most of history and throughout most of the world, God has been a mystery. In the days before the coming of Jesus (and most of history took place before the coming of Jesus), the only way to come to know God was to ask a Jew. And there were not a lot of Jews to ask. They were a little tiny country on the outskirts of the Roman Empire. They were not the chosen people because there were so many of them. They were a minority in a world full of majorities. But they had a special knowledge. To them God had revealed Himself. It was to them that God spoke through the prophets. When Jesus came, it was to preach, teach, and minister primarily among the Jews. As Paul opens this section of his epistle to the Ephesians, we will be reminded that the receivers of this epistle are mostly Gentiles, non-Jews.

THE MYSTERY INTRODUCED

> *For this reason I, Paul, the prisoner of Christ Jesus for the sake of you Gentiles -- 2 if indeed you have heard of the stewardship of God's grace which was given to me for you; 3 that by revelation there was made known to me the mystery, as I wrote before in brief. (Ephesians 3:1-3).*

Before introducing the mystery, Paul introduces himself - the steward of the mystery. The manner in which he introduces himself is striking. He introduces himself as *Paul, the prisoner of Christ Jesus*. What is so striking about this introduction is that, for the past two to four years Paul has been a prisoner of Rome. He was arrested in Jerusalem. And he was transported under guard to Caesarea. And then he was placed onto a prison ship and transported to Rome. He has now been in Rome for some time. He is a prisoner. He is under house arrest. But he describes himself as a prisoner, not of Rome or of the Empire, but of Jesus Christ.

> Paul begins by talking about "for this reason" – a phrase that expects a corresponding action on his part. But that action will not be given until verse 14. It is as though Paul interrupts himself.

Paul understands that all which has befallen him came first through a nail-scarred hand. He has been imprisoned in accordance with the plan and purpose of Jesus. This plan is *for the sake of you Gentiles*. It has been accomplished so that the gospel of Christ might be taken to the Gentiles throughout the Roman empire.

Indeed, it is in a very literal sense that Paul was a prisoner *for the sake of you Gentiles*. It had been over the very issue of allowing Gentiles into the church which had led to the riot in which Paul was originally arrested.

Paul had been preaching the gospel. The gospel which he proclaimed stated that a man could be accepted by God apart from the works of the Law - even a Gentile man.

Paul was a steward of that gospel. It was not a message which he had invented. He had not reasoned it out. Rather, it had been entrusted to him - made known to him *by revelation*. This is important. It means that Paul did not invent his gospel. It is not a gospel which is different from the gospel preached by Jesus. They preached the same gospel.

Every once in a while, I come across someone who teaches that Paul was just a crusty old woman-hater who spouted his own opinion on issues and that we ought to stick with the words of Jesus. This is not true. Paul's message and his teachings were given to him by revelation of the risen Jesus Himself.

THE MYSTERY HIDDEN

> *By referring to this, when you read you can understand my insight into the mystery of Christ, 5 which in*

> *other generations was not made known to the sons of men, as it has now been revealed to His holy apostles and prophets in the Spirit (Ephesians 3:4-5).*

Paul first mentioned this mystery in chapter 1. He mentioned it in 1:9 - *"He made known to us the mystery of His will."* It is a mystery which was given to him (3:3). That is significant because it had been previously hidden. That is what made it a mystery.

Other Generations	This Generation
Was not made known to the sons of men	Has now been revealed to His holy apostles and prophets in the Spirit.

Paul is going to share a mystery which was totally unknown in the Old Testament. What he gives to us was hidden from the fathers and the prophets. As great a prophet as was Moses or Elijah, neither of them knew of this truth. This means that, whatever this mystery is, it cannot have been something that was taught in the Old Testament.

Here is an amazing thing. While God was a mystery to most of the world and while the Jews had been entrusted with the oracles of God, there was something which was hidden even from the Jews.

THE MYSTERY EXPLAINED

> *To be specific, that the Gentiles are fellow heirs and fellow members of the body, and fellow partakers of the promise in Christ Jesus through the gospel (Ephesians 3:6).*

In order to explain what is the mystery, Paul does something unusual. He has not the words to express himself, so he coins his own words. He invents three words.

Greek Word	Translation	Meaning
Sugkleronoma	*Fellow heirs*	Has to do with possessions

Sussoma	*Fellow members of the body*	Reflects on our position
Summetocha	*Fellow partakers of the promise*	Has to do with power

What is the mystery? Before I tell you what it **is**, let me say what it is **not**. It is not the truth that the Gentiles would turn to God. That had been promised in the Old Testament. The prophet Isaiah said that the Messiah would be a light to the Gentiles.

The mystery is something greater. What can be greater than all the nations coming to know God? Here it is. Not only would the nations come to know Him, but both Gentiles and Jews would be joined in the closest possible bond.

1. Fellow Heirs.

    An heir is someone who inherits. The inheritance is the kingdom, promised from the Old Testament. It was an inheritance first promised to Abraham and then passed to his son and his son's son and to all Israel. Notice that there is not one kingdom for Jews and one kingdom for Gentiles. We have become fellow heirs.

2. Fellow members of the body.

    What is this body of which Paul speaks? I believe it to be the body of Christ. In 1 Corinthians 12:13 Paul says that *"by one Spirit were we all baptized into one body, whether we be Jews or Greeks, whether we be bond or free; and have been all made to drink into one Spirit."*

    There is nothing more unified than a body. Have you ever witnessed your hand having an argument with your foot? "Why do I have to be walked on all day? All I ever do is stand around in this smelly old sock while you get to write letters and play a guitar and shake other hands. No one ever wants to shake a foot. It's not fair!" Silly, isn't it? And the church is no less silly when we argue amongst ourselves. We are fellow members of the body.

3. Fellow partakers of the promise.

All of the promises of the New Covenant are yours to claim. What are the promises of the New Covenant?

> *"Behold, days are coming," declares the Lord, "when I will make a new covenant with the house of Israel and with the house of Judah, 32 not like the covenant which I made with their fathers in the day I took them by the hand to bring them out of the land of Egypt, My covenant which they broke, although I was a husband to them," declares the Lord.*
>
> *"But this is the covenant which I will make with the house of Israel after those days," declares the Lord, "I will put My law within them, and on their heart I will write it; and I will be their God, and they shall be My people.*
>
> *"And they shall not teach again, each man his neighbor and each man his brother, saying, 'Know the Lord,' for they shall all know Me, from the least of them to the greatest of them," declares the Lord, "for I will forgive their iniquity, and their sin I will remember no more." (Jeremiah 31:31-34).*

Notice the promises given by God to those who enter into the New Covenant.

- God's law written on the hearts of men.
- Relationship with God - He is their God and they are His people.
- A special and universal knowledge of God.
- Forgiveness of sins.

THE MYSTERY REVEALED

> *To be specific, that the Gentiles are fellow heirs and fellow members of the body, and fellow partakers of the promise in Christ Jesus through the gospel, 7 of which I was made a minister, according to the gift of God's grace which was given to me according to the working of His power. (Ephesians 3:6-7).*

God really has a sense of humor. Here was a Pharisee of the Pharisees who hated Gentiles and their culture. God appeared to him and said, "Go to the Gentiles." I imagine that Paul may have wanted to ask, "Can't I go to the Jews?" God would have answered, "No, Peter is already doing that."

The love of God overcame Paul's racism. He had come face to face with the grace of God. That confrontation changed his life. A confrontation with the Living God always has that effect.

Paul's appointment to ministry was *"according to the gift of God's grace which was given to me according to the working of His power."* Paul didn't become a minister because he was so faithful. Or because he was a good speaker. Or because he had a seminary education. Or because he was especially spiritual. It was because of grace.

Don't miss this! The same gracious principle that was involved in bringing you to salvation was involved in calling Paul into ministry. That same principle is involved in calling you into ministry, too.

What? Called into ministry? Yes. If you are a Christian, then you have been called into ministry. That doesn't mean you have to quit your job or go to seminary. But you are nonetheless a minister. The only question is what kind. Will you be faithful to the ministry to which you have been called? Will you hear the words of the Lord ultimately say, "Well done, good and faithful servant"?

THE MYSTERY ADMINISTERED

> *To me, the very least of all saints, this grace was given, to preach to the Gentiles the unfathomable riches of Christ, 9 and to bring to light what is the administration of the mystery which for ages has been hidden in God who created all things; 10 so that the manifold wisdom of God might now be made known through the church to the rulers and the authorities in the heavenly places. (Ephesians 3:8-10).*

The mystery is being revealed through the church. God is doing something special in His church. He is doing it for all the world to see. But that is not all. He is doing it, not only for the world to see, but also for the benefit of *"the rulers and the authorities in the heavenly places."*

This is amazing. It has been said that "all the world's a stage." There is some truth to that. The church is a stage. I don't mean the building. I mean the people inside the building. You are the stage. The world is watching you to see what Christ does in the life of a person.

The world is not the only one watching. Angels and rulers and heavenly beings are also watching. Beings so powerful and so majestic that, were one to appear, we would be sorely tempted to fall down and worship. But they are entranced with us. Not with us in ourselves, but in what Christ is doing in us.

THE MYSTERY APPLIED

This was in accordance with the eternal purpose which He carried out in Christ Jesus our Lord, 12 in whom we have boldness and confident access through faith in Him.
Therefore I ask you not to lose heart at my tribulations on your behalf, for they are your glory. (Ephesians 3:11-13).

Here is the point. These Ephesian Christians are in danger of becoming downhearted. Their founding pastor has been arrested and is in prison awaiting trial. The wheels of justice have ground to a halt. He is not only in prison, but he has been in prison for a long time. They hear what he is going through and they know that they might be next. They feel for him. They have prayed for him and it seems their prayers have not been answered.

They are beginning to wonder about it all. It appears that God's plan has failed. His apostle has been imprisoned. This time there has been no earthquake to open the cell doors and no angel to lead the prisoner to freedom. Years have passed and Paul is still chained, but Paul wants them to know that there is a divine purpose at work. Knowing that purpose results in boldness – even from a Roman prison. Paul's hardships have resulted in glorious growth.

It is easy to be faithful in the midst of obvious success. When the church is bursting at the seams. When your bank account is good. When Sunday school classes are full. When everything is going well.

Will you be faithful when you cannot see the immediate results? Will you be faithful to share the gospel when you do it and no one believes? Sunday school teachers, will you be faithful when there is just a small handful of students - when you can count their number on one hand and still have fingers to spare? Will you be faithful when you are the only one being faithful?

You will if you remember that there is an eternal purpose at work. Your faithfulness bears fruit, not necessarily today or tomorrow, but in eternity.

PAUL'S PRIESTLY PRAYER
Ephesians 3:14-21

The Bible has quite a lot to say on the subject of prayer. Jesus taught His disciples to pray and the Gospel of John contains an entire chapter of the prayer of Jesus to His Heavenly Father. There is one entire book of the Bible, the Psalms, that is devoted to the subject of prayer and that contains 150 separate prayers.

We don't normally think of the epistle to the Ephesians as an epistle of prayer, but perhaps we should. It contains two rather long prayers, one in the first chapter and one in chapter 3. These two prayers contain a number of stylistic similarities:

Ephesians 1:15-22	Ephesians 3:14-19
Paul prays that God would give to the Ephesians a spirit of wisdom and of revelation in the knowledge of Him	Paul prays that God would grant the Ephesians to be strengthened with power through His Spirit in the inner man
...so that they might know what is... • The hope of their calling • The riches of His inheritance • The greatness of His power	...so that they may be able to comprehend... • The breadth and length and height and depth • The love of Christ
...His body, the fulness of Him who fills all in all.	...so that you may be filled up to all the fulness of God.
The focus of the prayer is upon what the Ephesians will know.	The focus of the prayer is upon how the Ephesians will be empowered.

At the very heart of both of these prayers is a request that these believers might come to really know and experience the gospel. The point is that academic knowledge of the good news is not enough; you must also have an experiential encounter with that good news.

THE DIRECTION OF PAUL'S PRAYER

For this reason I bow my knees before the Father, 15 from whom every family in heaven and on earth derives its name (Ephesians 3:14-15).

Paul's prayer is directed toward the Father. That is the way Jesus taught His disciples to pray. He taught them to say, "Our Father who art in heaven..." He is the God of heaven and earth, the God of all creation, but He is also our Father if we have entered into His family through faith in His Son.

> Paul's words in describing the Father "from whom every family in heaven and on earth derives its name" stand in contrast to the claim of the worshipers in Artemis as recorded in Acts 19:27 – "she whom all of Asia and the world worship." You can go today to Ephesus where the Temple to Artemis once stood and you will find only a barren field.

In this case, Paul connects the idea of the fatherhood of God with the observation that it is from God that *every family in heaven and on earth derives its name.* It is true that God is the Father of the believer in a special sense, but here the focus is that God is the Father of all mankind. This is the same thing of which Paul described in his sermon in Athens when he said, to the pagan Greeks, "In Him we live and move and exist, as even some of your own poets have said, 'For we also are His children.'" (Acts 17:28).

The point is that we approach God as both our Father in the context of our new birth as well as in the context of the fact that He is our Creator and the Creator of all mankind. There is thus both a personal as well as a cosmic setting to this prayer.

THE DESIRE OF PAUL'S PRAYER

...that He would grant you, according to the riches of His glory, to be strengthened with power through His Spirit in the inner man (Ephesians 3:16).

Paul's prayer is that the church would be strengthened with power, not merely on the outside, but *in the inner man.* Our problem is that we are attracted to outward forms of power. We seek political power to change the laws of our nation to conform to that which is taught in the Scriptures. There is nothing wrong with such a desire. We ought to hunger for God's righteousness to fill the earth. But Paul's prayer is not for political power. Instead, he wants the church to be filled with an inward power that comes through the filling of the Spirit of God.

That is the kind of power Jesus promised. He told His disciples that the Spirit would come and that they would receive power to be witnesses throughout all the earth (Acts 1:8). They had no political power; the political powers were able to pass legislation that made it a crime to be a Christian. They had no financial power; they were known for their poverty. But they exercised a spiritual power that emboldened them to stand before all sorts of opposition that speak the name of Jesus. What took place for those twelve disciples, Paul wants for all the church.

Paul has already told the Ephesians of his prayer that they might come to know what is the surpassing greatness of God's power toward us who believe. (Ephesians 1:18-19). Now He prays that they might actually be strengthened with that same power. They have been told they have such power as a resource; now He prays that they might enjoy an experiential utilization of that power.

THE REASON FOR PAUL'S PRAYER

> *...so that Christ may dwell in your hearts through faith; and that you, being rooted and grounded in love, 18 may be able to comprehend with all the saints what is the breadth and length and height and depth, 19 and to know the love of Christ which surpasses knowledge, that you may be filled up to all the fullness of God. (Ephesians 3:17-19).*

Paul opened this section back in verse 14 with the words, "For this reason..." This entire section is given to explain the reason for Paul's prayer, but now as we come to verses 17-19, we arrive at the core of that reason. It is so that Christ would dwell in our hearts.

> The Greek text of verse 17 literally says, *"...so that Christ through faith may dwell in your hearts in love being rooted and grounded."* Since the original Greek text had no punctuation, it is not certain whether the phrase "in love" is to describe how Christ is to dwell in your heart or whether it speaks of that into which you are to be rooted and grounded. Most translations have adopted the former sense.

The promise of God to Abraham

and later to the nation of Israel was always that God would dwell with His people. That was what the tabernacle was all about. It was known as the Tent of Meeting, the place where God's presence would be manifested. It was located in the middle of the camp. God was with His people.

Paul wants to see the same thing in the church. He wishes to see Christ in the church in a very practical way. The way this will take place is as He dwells in the hearts of individual believers. This takes place as we trust in Him.

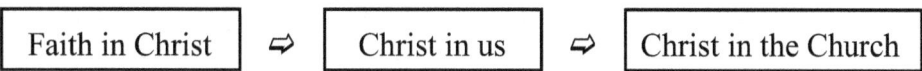

Notice that this is not described in terms of an artificial construct. It is likened to an organic process. He speaks of believers being rooted and grounded. Into what are we rooted and grounded? It is in Christ, but it is described here as being rooted and grounded in love. Our relationship with Christ is not described only in terms of faith, but also in terms of love. It is not a love that we generate among ourselves; it is a love that comes from Christ dwelling in our hearts and which results in our becoming even further acquainted with the love of Christ. Neither is that an end unto itself, for Paul goes on to show how the result of knowing the love of Christ is that we might be filled up to all the fullness of God.

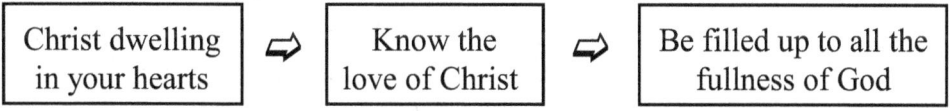

Remember the words of the preacher in the book of Ecclesiastes? He looked at all the world had to offer and he summarized it with a single word – emptiness. By contrast, the Christian life is a life of fullness. God wants to fill our lives with His fullness.

THE CONFIDENCE OF PAUL'S PRAYER

> *Now to Him who is able to do far more abundantly beyond all that we ask or think, according to the power that works within us, 21 to Him be the glory in the church and in Christ Jesus to all generations forever and ever. Amen. (Ephesians 3:14-21).*

As we come to these final verses of this section of Paul's epistle, we find that we have come full circle from where we began. Paul began his epistle with a doxology and we have returned to a doxology.

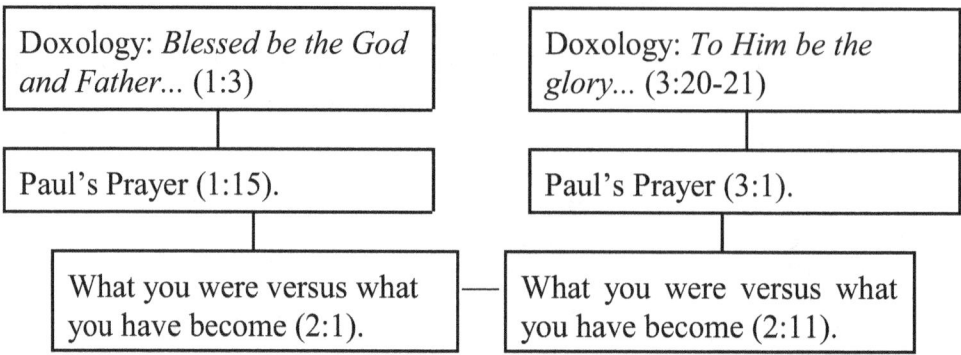

The opening words, "Now to Him who is able..." are used both here as well as in Paul's benediction in Romans 16:25 and also in the closing benediction in Jude 24. This doxology is given by way of a dedication. These words are meant to hold up and glorify the Lord, even as they are offered as a gift of worship to Him.

1. God is able to do something.

    When we read of "Him who is able," this speaks to the power and the ability of God. The reason for Paul's prayer is that God is able to answer. That is one of the primary reasons we pray. It is because we address the One who is able; the One who has the power over all things and who is able to meet our needs.

2. He is able to do what we ask.

    I am often asked about the value of prayer in light of the sovereignty of God. The question goes something like this: If God is completely sovereign and in control of the universe, knowing the end from the beginning and having planned out all events in history, then why should I pray? My reply is that since God is completely sovereign and in control of the universe, knowing and planning all things, then how can we not pray? The truth of the sovereignty of God serves as an impetus and a motivation for prayer. We pray because God is able to answer our prayers.

3. He is able to do immeasurably more than we can ask or think.

God is able to answer our prayers, but He is not limited by the limitations of our prayers. They are merely a starting point. His ability to act goes far beyond our ability to imagine.

The fact that this has application to us and not only to stained-glass saints of the Bible is seen in the phrase that it is "according to his power that is at work in us." This moves the blessings of this benediction from the theoretical to the practical. Paul is praying for that to take place which is already taking place.

The last portion of this doxology is markedly similar to the closing words of the Lord's Prayer as given in Matthew 6:13 – *For Yours is the kingdom and the power and the glory forever*. It is a call to worship the One who is worthy the eternal God of creation.

THE CHRISTIAN WALK
Ephesians 4:1-16

Ephesians 4 marks the pivotal point in this book. During the first three chapters, the believer is only told to do one thing, to believe what God has said about him. Throughout these first three chapters, God does all the work. You can do nothing. You can only learn about who you are in Christ. It is here that you learn that you have an identity in Christ Jesus. Because you have been identified with Him, you share in everything that He has.

- Because He is righteous, you have been declared to be righteous.
- Because He has eternal life, you share in that eternal life.
- Because He is an heir to the kingdom, you are a co-heir with Him.
- Because He rose from the dead, you will also have a bodily resurrection.
- This is your position in Christ.
- You are reckoned to be seated right now in heaven with Christ. All of the privileges of heaven are yours now.

The plea throughout the first three chapters of Ephesians has been that you believe these things. But now as we come to chapter 4, there is a change. There is a call to action.

> *Therefore I, the prisoner of the Lord, entreat you to walk in a manner worthy of the calling with which you have been called, 2 with all humility and gentleness, with patience, showing forbearance to one another in love, 3 being diligent to preserve the unity of the Spirit in the bond of peace. (Ephesians 4:1-3).*

This passage begins with the word "therefore." This takes us back to the last three chapters that have gone on before. Paul is about to give us some instructions for living. But he has already laid the foundation as to why we ought to live that way. Everything that he will say from this

> Paul says, *"I... **call** you to walk in a manner worthy of the **calling** with which you have been **called**."*

point forward is based upon the truths set forth in the first three chapters.

Paul refers to himself as *the prisoner of the Lord*. This is significant. It is significant because of where Paul was as he penned these words. He was a prisoner in Rome. And he had been a prisoner for a long time.

Picture the scene. Paul is in Rome under house arrest. An iron chain runs from a ring set into a wall to one made fast around his ankle. A soldier stands nearby on guard. It is his job to guard this old Jewish man. He is guarding a prisoner of the Roman Empire.

The old man is writing a letter. It is already several pages in length. Notice what he does not write. He does not call himself a prisoner of Rome. He sees himself as a prisoner, not of Rome, but of the Lord Jesus Christ. He realizes that God is in control of his circumstances. What are your circumstances? Have you come to the realization that, no matter what they appear to be, God is still in control?

Paul could have worded this in the terms of a command. After all, he was an apostle. He had the authority to command the church. But he does not do that. Instead he makes an entreaty. He pleads with these believers. His desire is that they live in a manner that is consistent with what they already are in Christ. He has spent the last three chapters telling them what they are in Christ. Now he calls them to live according to that new identity.

Ephesians 4:1-16 is organized in a large parallel known as a *chiasm*. The first part of this parallel (verses 1-6) deals with the unity of the church. The second part of this parallel (verses 7-16) deals with the diversity of the church.

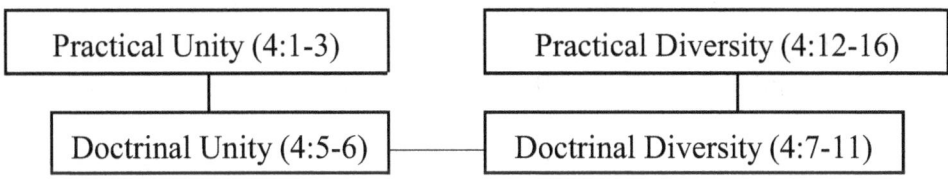

PRESERVING THE UNITY

> *Therefore I, the prisoner of the Lord, entreat you to walk in a manner worthy of the calling with which you have*

> *been called, 2 with all humility and gentleness, with patience, showing forbearance to one another in love, 3 being diligent to preserve the unity of the Spirit in the bond of peace. (Ephesians 4:1-3).*

Notice that we are not instructed to make the unity. Instead we are told to preserve the unity and to guard it. There exists a unity among believers. This is not something that we have generated ourselves. It is a unity which is based upon the Lord and who He is and what He has done.

You cannot make this unity. But if you are not careful, you can damage it. You can damage it when you do not show...

- All humility.
- Gentleness.
- Patience.
- Forbearance to one another in love.

> A high calling does not justify a haughty attitude. We are called to humility.

THE BASIS OF UNITY

> *There is one body and one Spirit, just as also you were called in one hope of your calling; 5 one Lord, one faith, one baptism, 6 one God and Father of all who is over all and through all and in all. (Ephesians 4:4-6).*

As we read through this passage, we see the repetition of one particular word. It is the word "one." It is used seven times in these three short verses. Whenever you see repetition used in the Bible, it is there for a reason. It is not that Paul needed some filler between verses 3 and 7. It is that he wanted to make a point. When you see this kind of repetition, it is used for emphasis.

Paul wants to emphasize our "oneness." When I use words like "oneness" and "unity" I do not mean that we all have to be the same. I am not saying that to be spiritual you have to walk like me and talk like me and dress like me. All too often, this concept of unity is taught in the form of a cookie-cutter Christianity in which you have to always be saying Christian things and wearing Christian clothes and singing Christian songs and eating Christian cookies. We have tried to remake one another in those kinds of images where you must be just like each other to fit into our preconceived idea of what a Christian ought to be.

When Paul comes to verse 7, he will explain to the Ephesians how, in the midst of their oneness, God has made them different. We have different backgrounds and come from different cultures. God has gifted us with different gifts. But with all that diversity, we are still one.

This unity is based upon Christ and your identification with Him. It is the unity which you share by virtue of your position in Him. This is shown in the continuing repetition of the word "one."

- One body
- One Spirit
- One hope
- One Lord
- One faith
- One baptism
- One God and Father

Notice the three members of the Godhead who are mentioned throughout this unity. God Himself is at the center of the unity to which we are called. He is One and He calls us to be one.

Holy Spirit	**Son**	**Father**
One body One Spirit One hope	One Lord One faith One baptism	One God and Father

This is the basis of fellowship between believers. What does "fellowship" mean? It means to have things in common. True Christian fellowship does not depend upon financial status or age or cultural background. We have something much greater in common with one another. What we have in common is eternal. It is our position in Christ.

Now we come to a crucial question. How are we to preserve this unity? What can we do to accomplish this preservation? It is first by being "in Christ." He is the source of our unity. As we have become united to Him through faith, then we have also become united to all of His people. But that is not all. It is also by recognizing the fact that we are different.

The world typically tries to achieve unity by making everyone the same. That has been the strategy used by the communist governments of the 20th century. The thinking was that if everyone could be made to be the same, then everyone would get along. It did not work because it failed to see that we are different.

By contrast, Christianity shows that there are areas of similarities that make us one, but also that there are areas where God has made us different. This will be seen in the following verses.

GRACE - THE SOURCE OF OUR DIVERSITY

> *But to each one of us grace was given according to the measure of Christ's gift. 8 Therefore it says, "When he ascended on high, he led captive a host of captives, and he gave gifts to men." (Ephesians 4:7-8).*

Now we move from unity to diversity. We have a unity that is rooted in Christ, but we also have a diversity that is rooted in Christ. It is a diversity based on the fact that Christ has given various gifts to men.

There are two words here that go together. They are the noun "grace" and the verb "given." Grace is always something which is given and received. Grace involves the giving and receiving of a gift. You know what a gift is. A gift is something that you are given and which expects no repayment. You do not buy a gift or repay it. That would make it a purchase or a loan. A gift, by its very nature, expects no repayment.

When Christ died upon the cross, it was to provide us with the gift of eternal life. But that is not all. He also provided gifts for this life. This was promised in the Old Testament.

*Thou hast ascended on high,
Thou hast led captive Thy captives,
Thou hast received gifts among men,
Even among the rebellious also, that the Lord God may dwell there. (Psalm*

> Paul paraphrases Psalm 68:18 that says, *Thou hast received gifts among men.* Hendriksen makes the following observation: "The giving is implied in the receiving. When Christ ascended he was not returning to heaven with empty hands. On the contrary, as a result of accomplished mediatorial work he returned in triumph to heaven, in full possession of salvation for his people." (1989:191).

68:18).

This is the language of a triumph. In ancient times, a conquering general returning home would enjoy the honor of a triumph, a tumultuous parade. He would come through the gates of the city riding upon a white horse. Behind him in chains would come all those whom he had conquered in battle. It was a joyous time; a time when gifts were given and received.

This picture is of Jesus. He is the one who has conquered sin and death. He is the conquering King. When He did His work of providing for our salvation, He also went on to give gifts to His church. This was promised in the Old Testament:

> *Therefore, I will allot Him a portion with the great,*
> *And He will divide the booty with the strong;*
> *Because He poured out Himself to death,*
> *And was numbered with the transgressors;*
> *Yet He Himself bore the sins of many,*
> *And interceded for the transgressors. (Isaiah 53:12).*

The words of Isaiah are striking. They tell of how Christ won the victory and we get to participate in the booty. He did the fighting and we get the rewards.

There is a popular theory taught today in Christian circles that says during the Old Testament era people did not go to heaven but instead went to some temporary "compartment" and that when Christ ascended into heaven He took all of these people up into heaven with Him. But this is not the picture behind the phrase, "He led captivity captive." The Old Testament saints were not captives and being brought to heaven is not captivity.

This is a figure of speech that describes the conquest of an enemy. And that is what Jesus accomplished upon the cross. It was there that He defeated the devil and death and sin. As a result of these conquests, He now gives gifts to men. We will look at some of those gifts in just a moment, but first Paul takes a parenthetical excursus to further explain what Christ has done.

AN EXPLANATORY EXCURSUS

> *Now this expression, "He ascended," what does it*
> *mean except that He also had descended into the lower parts*

of the earth? 10 He who descended is Himself also He who ascended far above all the heavens, so that He might fill all things. (Ephesians 4:9-10).

Paul takes a moment to explain the Psalm which he quoted. He takes the first phrase of the Psalm - *"He ascended."* The subject of that Psalm is God. He is the One who is said to be ascending.

You've heard the old saying, "Whatever goes up must come down." But it is the exact opposite when you speak of God. You don't speak of God as being down here - you speak of Him being "up there." Indeed, the Hebrew word for "heaven" (שָׁמַיִם – *shamayim*) simply means, "Up there places" (שָׁם – *sham* is the word for "there"). When you speak of God ascending, that means that He had to have first descended. When it comes to God, whoever goes up must have first come down.

Here is the principle. The fact that God was described as ascending means that the Scriptures indicated that God would come to earth. He accomplished this in the person of Jesus Christ.

The reference to *into the lower parts of the earth* is simply a way of saying, "Down here" as opposed to "Up there." There was a time when Christ could not ascend into heaven. It was before the incarnation. He could not ascend into heaven because He was already in heaven. But then He came to earth to be born as a man. After His death, burial and resurrection, Jesus ascended *far above all the heavens*. He who became the lowest has now risen to become the very highest.

THE GOAL OF GROWTH

And He gave some as apostles, and some as prophets, and some as evangelists, and some as pastors and teachers, 12 for the equipping of the saints for the work of service, to the building up of the body of Christ; 13 until we all attain to the unity of the faith, and of the knowledge of the Son of God, to a mature man, to the measure of the stature which belongs to the fullness of Christ. (Ephesians 4:11-13).

Now we come back to the topic at hand. Paul has been speaking of certain gifts which were given by Christ. They are spiritual gifts. This brings us to a question. What is a spiritual gift?

Before I state what it is, perhaps I should say what it is not. It is not an office in the church. It is not a natural talent, such as music or art. It is not a reward. A spiritual gift is a God-given ability for service. In this simple definition, we see three concepts.

- They are God-given: This is their Source.
- They involve an ability: This is their Meaning.
- They are for service: This is their Purpose.

Paul is not going to speak about spiritual gifts in general. Instead his focus is upon several very specific types of gifts. They are gifts involving communication.

Apostles	Leadership over all of the churches	Temporary
Prophets	Proclaimers of the word of God	
Evangelists	Proclaimers of the gospel	Permanent
Pastors & Teachers	Leading and teaching over individual churches	

1. Apostles.

    Our English word "apostle" comes from the Greek *apostolos* (ἀπόστολος). It is an old military term, going back to the days of the Peloponnesian War between Athens and Sparta. The *apostolos* was the admiral of the fleet. He was the supreme commander. He was the one who had been sent out by the rulers of the city to wield authority over the Athenian navy.

    The New Testament usage is similar. The apostles were those men who had been commissioned by Jesus Christ to wield authority over the churches of God.

2. Prophets.

    Prophets were familiar in Old Testament times. But there are also examples in the book of Acts of New Testament prophets. Like their Old Testament counterparts, they were given the ability both to foretell and to forth tell the message of God.

I do not believe that there are apostles and prophets today in the same sense that there were in the days in which the New Testament was written. These two gifts were temporary. They were gifts which were given for the establishment of the early church. And after the church was established and the Scriptures had been given, these two gifts ceased to be given.

There are two more gifts. These gifts are also given for the establishment of the church. It is the use of these two gifts which take up the slack left by the absence of the apostles and prophets.

3. Evangelists.

The word "evangelist" literally means, "messenger of good news." An evangelist is one who has been gifted with the ability to share the gospel clearly so that it will be understood and accepted by others. This is not to say that you must have the gift of evangelism in order to share the gospel. Rather it means that certain people have a special gift which gives them greater ability in bringing others to Christ.

4. Pastors and Teachers.

There are two parts to this gift. The first part is the aspect of the Pastor. The word "pastor" simply means "shepherd." He is one who shepherds and cares for the flock of God. The second part of this gift is that of "teacher." He is one who is able to explain the Word of God in a way in which it can be understood. It reminds me of the young man who was certain that he had the gift of teaching. Unfortunately no one else had the gift of listening.

Now we must be careful here. We must be careful not to confuse the gift of pastor-teacher with an office of position within the church. The Bible indicates that the early church was under the leadership of a plurality of elders. Each local church had several mature and spiritual men who had the responsibility of leading the church. They were called "elders" or "overseers." Never does the Bible say that all pastor-teachers are to be elders or that all elders are to be pastor-teachers.

Our tendency is to look for gifted men to rule the church. But the Biblical mandate is that we look for spiritual men to rule over the church.

In verse 12, we are given the reason for these particular spiritual gifts. It is introduced by the word "for." This clause sets forth the purpose for which God has given apostles and prophets and evangelists and pastors and teachers.

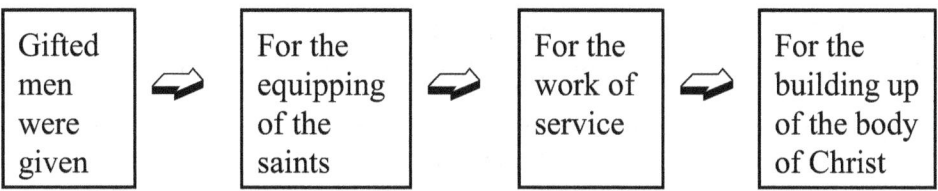

The immediate reason for the gifts of communication (evangelist and pastor-teacher) is to equip believers for the work of service. Most people do not seem to know this. Most people seem to think that it is only those who have the gifts of evangelism and pastor-teacher who are to do the work of service and the work of ministry.

The church is often run like a spectator sport. Football is a spectator sport – twenty two men who desperately need rest being watched by twenty two thousand people who desperately need exercise. People come to watch the pastor "do his thing" and they think that their part is to be quiet and to listen and his part is to minister. But Christianity is not a spectator sport. All Christians are called to do the work of ministry.

The preposition which introduces the clause "for the work of service" is noteworthy. It is the preposition εἰς (*eis*). It is normally translated "into." It is the equipped saints who are to go into the work of service. We often speak of one who is going into the ministry. This is wrong. All believers are to be in ministry.

The ultimate purpose of this progression is *to the building up of the body of Christ*. This is a reference to the edification of the church. The church is involved in a building program. This building program is twofold.

- Initially, it involves bringing the unsaved to Christ.

This is the area in which the evangelist is instrumental in equipping the saints.

- Then it involves the teaching and maturing of those who have come to Christ in faith. This is the area of the pastor-teacher.

The result is that *we all attain to the unity of the faith, and of the knowledge of the Son of God, to a mature man, to the measure of the stature which belongs to the fullness of Christ* (4:13).

We saw in verse 3 the plea to preserve the unity of the Spirit. It was to this end that the gifts were given to the church. This was their purpose - the attainment of a mature unity - that we be like Christ.

Verse 11	Verse 12	Verse 13
Gifts were given	For the building up of the body	Until we all attain to the fulness of Christ
Past	Present	Future

THE RESULT OF GROWTH

As a result, we are no longer to be children, tossed here and there by waves and carried about by every wind of doctrine, by the trickery of men, by craftiness in deceitful scheming; 15 but speaking the truth in love, we are to grow up in all aspects into Him who is the head, even Christ, 16 from whom the whole body, being fitted and held together by what every joint supplies, according to the proper working of each individual part, causes the growth of the body for the building up of itself in love. (Ephesians 4:14-16).

As the passage continues, we are given a series of causes and effects that least us to realize what is the result of Christian growth.

Verse 14	Verse 15	Verse 16
The negative result	The Positive result	How that result is achieved

| Tossed about children | Growing up into Christ | By all members pulling together in love |

1. *We are no longer to be children* (4:14).

    There is nothing wrong with being a child. Being a child is a natural phase of growth. But when many years have passed and there is nothing in the way of growth, then something is seriously wrong.

    One of the marks of a child is given in the rest of this verse. It is his reaction to false teaching. He is easily swayed by every sort of teaching. Just like a child runs from one toy to the next, so also a new believer is easily moved from one doctrine to the next.

2. *Tossed here and there by waves and carried about by every wind of doctrine* (4:14).

    This is one of the marks of the immature believer. His faith is only as strong as the last good sermon he heard. The problem is one of spiritual discernment. Because he has not yet developed spiritual discernment, he cannot see the hazardous currents of false doctrine and soon he finds himself adrift. Many believers wind up as spiritual pinball machines, bouncing from one type of false teaching to another.

    What is the answer? Get with the Book. Get with true teaching. It is only as you feed upon the word of God that you can begin to develop spiritual discernment.

3. Speaking the truth in love (4:15).

    We are to be people of truth. The Greek text does not actually use the word "speaking." Instead we have the present participle of αληθευω (*aletheuo*). It is a word that means, "to tell the truth," but we could actually translate it as "truthing." We are to be such people of the truth that our lives are to be characterized as "truthing."

    Neither is this a selfish or a tactless truth-telling. We are to be people of truth and of love. That means I am to tell the truth is such a way as to show real love and concern for others.

4. *We are to grow up in all aspects into Him who is the head, even Christ* (4:15).

Here is the result of spiritual growth. The picture is of a body. The head of the body is Jesus Christ. The members are different aspects of the church. You are a vital part of that body. You are in a vital union with that body - but only insofar as you are in contact with the head.

What happens when the members of a human body doesn't receive or respond to messages from the brain? Paralysis. And the church is paralyzed when it is not in contact with its Head.

Verse 14	**Verse 15**
Children	Mature
Tossed about - unstable like waves	Grown up - stable like a building
In error	"Truthing in love"

Did you ever notice that the head of a child is much bigger in proportion to the rest of his body. The remainder of a child's life is spent in having his body catch up with his head. It is a fitting analogy, for that is how we spend the rest of our spiritual life here on earth. We are on a quest to catch up with our Head.

5. *From whom the whole body, being fitted and held together by what every joint supplies, according to the proper working of each individual part (4:16).*

Notice what holds the body together. It is not a single member. It is not those members with the gifts of evangelist or pastor-teacher. It is the unity of all the members.

This brings us full circle. Paul began with a call to preserve the unity that we have in Christ. Now we see that it is we who are in Christ who hold that unity together. It is only as each member of the body of Christ pulls together that this unity is preserved. And the result? The growth of the body.

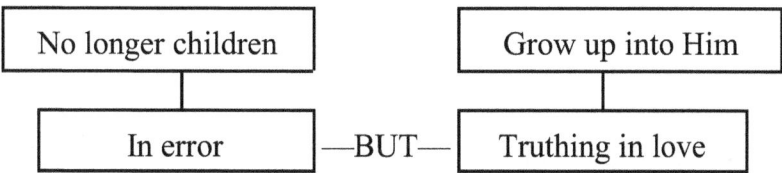

Are you in the body of Christ? I am not asking whether you are a member of a church or some particular denomination. I am asking if you have ever come to Christ, trusting Him as your Lord and Savior, giving your life to Him that He might give His life to you. If you have not, then I invite you to come to Him today.

But I also have another question. It is a question for Christians. Are you functioning within the body of Christ? Are you an active part of a local church? Not merely "on the roles," but participating in the nurture and growth of the entire body? You have a high calling and I call you to walk worthy of the calling with which you have been called.

CHRISTOLOGICAL IMPLICATIONS
Ephesians 4:17-24

Ephesians 4:1 was a pivotal point in Paul's epistle to the Ephesians. It was introduced by the word "therefore." Up to that point, he had spent three chapters telling the Ephesians what God had done for them. Now, on the basis of all that he had said, he called them to walk in accordance with that calling. In the verses which followed, he set forth what that calling was to be.

- It was a calling to unity (4:1-6).
- It was a calling of diversity (4:7-16).

The result of that calling was that believers might be built up in love through the working of the body to become like Christ. This has been the big picture, the bird's eye view. But now it is time to get practical. It is time to ask, "How do I fit into this big picture?" In this section, Paul presents a series of personal conclusions of how we are to live as a result of our position in Christ.

BECAUSE YOU ARE NOW IN CHRIST, YOU ARE TO WALK DIFFERENTLY

> *This I say therefore, and affirm together with the Lord, that you walk no longer just as the Gentiles also walk, in the futility of their mind (Ephesians 4:17).*

Paul is speaking to a primarily Gentile group. They had formerly lived a lifestyle of paganism. They had been involved in all of the vices that afflict our society today. But Paul does not place their former life on a plane any lower than his own.

> *And you were dead in your trespasses and sins, 2 in which you formerly walked according to the course of this*

> *world, according to the prince of the power of the air, of the spirit that is now working in the sons of disobedience. 3 Among them we too ALL formerly lived in the lusts of our flesh, indulging the desires of the flesh and of the mind, and were by nature children of wrath, even as the rest (Ephesians 2:1-3).*

Do you see it in verse 3? He says, "We all formerly lived that way." Jew and Gentile, religious and pagan, it makes no difference. Before you came to Christ, you lived in a way that pleased you. You were the lord of your life and the captain of your soul. But now there has come a change. You have sworn allegiance to another. You have proclaimed Him both Savior and Lord.

Because of that, you are now called to live differently than the rest of the world. This is no easy task. It is not easy because you still live in the world. But the solution is not getting the world to live like Christians, it is in getting Christians to stop living like the world. You do that and then you will begin to impact the world.

BECAUSE YOU ARE NOW IN CHRIST, YOU ARE TO SEE THE LIGHT

> *...being darkened in their understanding, excluded from the life of God because of the ignorance that is in them... (Ephesians 4:18a).*

What is darkness? It has no quality of its own. Darkness is simply the absence of light. In this passage, light and darkness are being used as symbols for knowledge and ignorance. When you go into a dark room, there may be all sorts of wondrous things there, but you cannot see them. It is only when you turn on the lights that you can see. Darkness brings about ignorance.

> Notice the correlation between life and light. It takes us back to the words of John 1:4 - "In Him was life; and the life was the light of men."

Light, on the other hand, reveals. It is when the lights are on that you can see things as they really are. There is less chance of walking into something and hurting yourself.

This tells me something about spiritual living. In order to be right, we must think right. What you think about is what you will soon become. There is a connection between thought and life.

I've lived most of my life in south Florida. Big cities that never sleep. Streetlights. At night it is never really dark. But there have been occasions where I've visited the open country. I used to have family in the Ozark Mountains of northwestern Arkansas, twenty five miles from the nearest city. You go out at night and the sky is filled with stars. Thousands of points of light. What happens in the city? The stars are still there, but they are so dim in contrast to the lights of the city that they are invisible.

There is a lesson here. It is that when it is dark enough, a even little light will do. Are you the only Christian in your workplace? That is too bad. No, that's good! Because your little light can now be seen in the darkness. Are your neighbors all pagans? Drinking beer on Saturday night and mowing their lawns on Sunday? They can see your little light by way of contrast. Are you the only Christian in your family? Are you facing relatives that think you've become some sort of religious fanatic? Be encouraged; your little light is making a difference.

BECAUSE YOU ARE NOW IN CHRIST, YOU ARE TO BE TENDER-HEARTED

> *...because of the hardness of their heart; 19 and they, having become callous, have given themselves over to sensuality for the practice of every kind of impurity with greediness. (Ephesians 4:18b-19).*

In my younger days, I used to play the guitar quite well. In those days, I would practice several times a week. In doing so, the fingers on my left hand became calloused. The skin on my fingertips became hardened to the touch of the strings. It is a good thing when your fingers get hardened. It is a bad thing when your heart gets hardened. How does it happen?

When you sin, it results in a pricked conscience. You know that it is wrong and you know that you ought to do right. And your sense of "ought" screams out at you. At this point, you have one of two options. You can either...

- Listen to your conscience.
- Ignore your conscience.

If you listen to your conscience, it will remain tender and open and ready to operate in the future. But if you ignore your conscience, then the next time it will not bother you so much. Here is Paul's point. It is possible to be so hardened that your conscience no longer troubles you, even though you might engage in the most vile sin imaginable.

BECAUSE YOU ARE NOW IN CHRIST, YOU ARE TO ACT LIKE CHRIST

But you did not learn Christ in this way (Ephesians 4:20).

Notice how Paul turns this phrase. He does not speak of how you learned about Christ. He speaks of how you learned Christ. There is a lesson here. Christianity is more that a mere series of theological points. Christianity involves a person. Don't get me wrong, theology is important. But much more important is the person of Christ. It is possible to learn all sorts of things about Christ without ever learning Christ. What does it mean to "learn Christ?" It means to be like Him.

It is the language of an actor. An actor is one who takes on the role of another. He plays a part. To play the part, you have to learn the part. I once watched one of our deacons do a characterization of a current presidential candidate. It was quite funny. In doing so, he had learned to mimic that candidate. Similarly, we are called to mimic Jesus Christ, not as a part of a comic routine, but because He is the model for which that which we are to be. Indeed, Paul is going to say this very thing in the next chapter: "Be imitators of Christ" (Ephesians 5:1). How do you do that? By learning Christ. Study Him. Get to know Him. As you get to know Him, you will come to love Him. And as you come to love Him, His very character will be reproduced in your life.

Are you learning Christ? Are you seeking to follow Him in order to be like Him? This is the essence of discipleship. Jesus said that the goal of a disciple is to be like his teacher (Matthew 10:25).

BECAUSE YOU ARE NOW IN CHRIST, YOU ARE TO LIVE WITHOUT PRESUMPTION

But you did not learn Christ in this way, 21 if indeed you have heard Him and have been taught in Him, just as truth is in Jesus (Ephesians 4:20-21).

Paul has been speaking to the members of the Ephesian church as though they are Christians. I have been doing the same thing to you. And yet, we are not to presume upon the grace of God.

You are a Christian if you have...
- Heard Him, and...
- Been taught in Him, and...
- Believed in Him, and...
- Determined to follow Him.

Paul warns believers to *"test yourselves to see if you are in the faith; examine yourselves! Or do you not recognize this about yourselves that Jesus Christ is in you - unless indeed you fail the test"* (2 Corinthians 13:5).

At the same time, you should realize that this conditional clause assumes the integrity of those who hear. In the Greek language, it is possible to say, "if" and mean four different things. There are four different types of conditional clauses in Greek.

1. First class condition: Assumed to be true.
   "If" and it is true. Satan says this to Jesus: *"If you are the Son of God..."*

2. Second class condition: Assumed to be false.
   "If" and it is not true. Satan uses this one of Jesus: *"If you will fall down and worship me (but you won't)..."*

3. Third class condition: Assumption of uncertainty.
   "If" and maybe it is true and maybe it is not.
   "If you confess your sins (maybe you will and maybe you won't)..."

4. Fourth class condition: Assumption of desire.
 "If" and it is not true, but it is desired to be.

It is the first class condition which is used here. Paul assumes that they are believers. He takes their faith at face value. You see, it is not my job to judge your heart. That is your job. You are to consider yourself as to whether you are truly in the faith. You ask yourself *if indeed you have heard Him and have been taught in Him.*

BECAUSE YOU ARE NOW IN CHRIST, YOU ARE TO EXHIBIT A RENEWED NATURE

> *That, in reference to your former manner of life, you lay aside the old self, which is being corrupted in accordance with the lusts of deceit, 23 and that you be renewed in the spirit of your mind (Ephesians 4:22-23).*

Notice the realm of your renewal. It is in *the spirit of your mind.* This takes in the whole man. It is not just his mind - it is more than mere intellectual assent. But it is also more than a spiritual renewal which does not impact your thinking or your daily lifestyle. It is a complete renewal. There are two possible extremes to which we can go. They are illustrated in this chart.

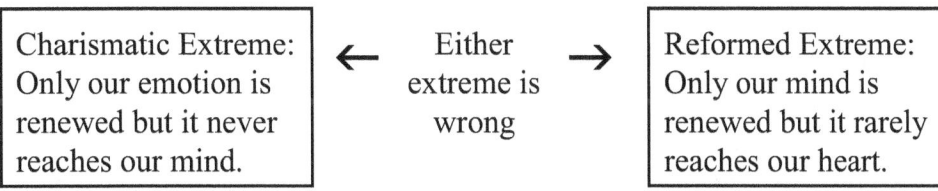

A conversion which has touched your mental faculties but which has not touched your heart is no conversion at all. And a conversion which has played with your emotional heartstrings but which has not been founded upon the propositional truths of the gospel will give no foundation upon which to build.

BECAUSE YOU ARE NOW IN CHRIST, YOU ARE TO PUT ON CHRIST

> *...that, in reference to your former manner of life, you lay aside the old self, which is being corrupted in accordance with the lusts of deceit...* 24 *and put on the new self, which in the likeness of God has been created in righteousness and holiness of the truth. (Ephesians 4:22, 24).*

Do you remember the story that Jesus told of a wedding feast? The story is told in Matthew 22:1-13. It is a story of a king. This king was going to throw a wedding for his son. The invitations went out for all the guests to attend. But instead of guests, the king received excuses. And they were not very good excuses. People were just to busy to be bothered with affairs of the kingdom. To make matters worse, some of the messengers of the king were mistreated and even killed. And so, the king extended the invitation to all who might attend. The down and out. The bad and the good. Whosoever will was permitted to come.

But then a curious thing happened. As the king came to the feast, he spotted one particular guest who had come without a wedding garment. It was a formal affair and he had attended in cutoffs and a t-shirt. It was an insult to the honor of the king. And the man who so insulted the king was bound hand and foot and cast into outer darkness.

Here we see a corresponding call. It is not couched in the language of wedding garments. But it is given in that which you take off and that which you put on. There are two type of garments.

The Old Self	**The New Self**
Your former manner of life	The new life in Christ
On its way to destruction	Created anew
Rotting under the power of lust	Increasing under the power of God
Controlled by lust	Controlled by truth

Notice that Paul does not merely state this in terms of the negative. He does not say, "Take off the old self" and leave it at that. We are not called to remain spiritually naked. There is no neutral position.

That is the call of the world. The world likes to claim for itself neutrality.

I hear parents say, "I am not going to teach my child about God because I want him, when he is older, to make his own decision." Such a decision is not neutral - it is a stance in atheism. There is no neutrality when it comes to Christ. You are either for Him or else you are against Him.

Just as the king in Jesus' parable demanded a wedding garment of all who were in attendance, you are called to put on the new self. Here is the point.

- Jesus demands the new garment.
- Jesus is the new garment.

How do you receive this garment? How do you put it on and wear it? It is by faith. You might be thinking, "John, my faith isn't all that strong." That is okay. You take what faith you have to Him and ask Him to increase it. It is like the man who said, "Lord, I believe; help Thou my unbelief!" You take your faith to Him. Then look, not at your faith, but at Jesus.

THE RIGHT & THE WRONG OF IT
Ephesians 4:25-32

In Ephesians 4:1 we were introduced to the first command given in this entire epistle. Prior to that, Paul had told us everything that Christ has already done for us. But at the beginning of chapter 4 there was a change. We were told to do something. We were told to "walk in a manner worthy of the calling with which you have been called."

Having said that, he went on to show us the basis of that calling, that it if fulfilled as we walk in unity and recognize the diversity of spiritual gifts that have been given so that we work together in building up the body of Christ in love. But to tell you the truth, that is all very theoretical. It is Christianity laid out in its grand scheme of how things work. It is the bird's eye view of the Christian life. Now Paul takes those high and lofty goals and brings them down to earth. He comes to where we live and makes it very practical.

Paul accomplishes this goal with a series of commands. Most of them are rooted in the Ten Commandments, but there will be an important difference. While the Ten Commandments begin in our relationship with God and have that relationship as the subject of the first four of their number, these commands will be primarily focused upon how we are to relate with other people.

Most of these commands are going to be stated both negatively as well as positively. We will be told what we are to avoid and we will also be told what to embrace.

Negative	Positive
Lay aside falsehood	Speak truth
Do not steal	Labor so you can share
Avoid rotten speech	Speak words of edification

YOU ARE WARNED AGAINST LYING

Therefore, laying aside falsehood, speak truth each one of you with his neighbor, for we are members of one another. (Ephesians 4:25).

This section begins with the word "therefore." It directs our attention back to the previous verse. In verse 24, we were told to *put on the new self, which in the likeness of God has been created in righteousness and holiness of the truth.* Because we have been created in truth, we are to lay aside falsehood and to speak truth. As Paul states this command in both the negative as well as in the positive, we are meant to see it in view of a contrast.

Lay Aside Falsehood	Speak Truth with your Neighbor
The Old Self	The New Self
The way you were	The way you now are to be

Lying is wrong. But this command goes further than a simple command to abstain from deliberately lying. It calls us to be intentional in our truth-telling. Notice there is no reference here to big lies or to little white lies. There are no grey areas mentioned here; we are to be truthful in everything we say.

One of my pet peeves is to receive one of those Emails that have been passed along that contains an "urban legend," something that sounds true, but when you check it out, it turns to be unsubstantiated. It demonstrates a lack of integrity to pass along such reports when we have not taken care to check out its truth. We are to tell the truth and we ought to make sure that what we say is indeed the truth.

However, the focus here is not merely upon telling the truth about news reports or about our family or about our business dealings. It does not exclude such instances, but Paul has already been speaking in this chapter about the truth that is in Jesus (Ephesians 4:21). We are to speak truth to others about Jesus. We are to do that by sharing the gospel with those who do not know it and we are to remind one another of the gospel as we speak to our fellow Christians.

Negative	Neutral	Positive
Lies	Does not lie	Speaks truth

This sets forth a pattern that we shall see in a number of cases throughout the remainder of this chapter. We will be told to move, not merely away from that which is negative, but to embrace that which is positive.

Paul adds that *we are members of one another*. Is this reference to "one another" speaking only of other Christians, or is it a larger reference to our connectedness to all humanity? Normally such references in Paul's writings seem to focus upon the fellowship we have as Christians (Ephesians 4:2; 4:32; 5:19; 5:21). There is a connectedness we share as Christians that calls us to accountable living and accountable speaking.

YOU ARE WARNED AGAINST ANGER

> *Be angry, and yet do not sin; do not let the sun go down on your anger, 27 and do not give the devil an opportunity. (Ephesians 4:26-27).*

Most scholars agree that Paul is quoting from the Old Testament. The quote is taken from the Psalms.

> *Oh sons of men, how long will my honor become a reproach?*
> *How long will you love what is worthless and aim at deception?*
> *Selah.*
> *But know that the Lord has set apart the godly man for Himself;*
> *The Lord hears when I call to Him.*
> **Tremble**, *and do not sin;*
> *Meditate in your heart upon your bed, and be still. Selah. (Psalm 4:2-4).*

The word which the New American Standard Version translates "tremble" is taken from the root *ragaz*. It's literal meaning is "to tremble or quake." But when it refers to a person, its speaks of strong emotions. Those emotions can be fear. They can be worshipful awe before the presence of the Lord. Or they can be anger.

There is a lesson here. It is a lesson about emotions. Emotions are not sinful or wrong. The Lord made us to be emotional creatures. Some of us are more emotional than others. And that is okay. I come from a church tradition that has often fallen short in worshiping God with our emotions. Perhaps it is in reaction to that brand of Christianity which goes to emotional excess, where theology and truth are traded in for an emotional roller coaster ride of warm fuzzies. I am not advocating such excess. But I cannot help but think that we have gone too far in the other direction. Emotions are good. We are commanded to love the Lord, not just with our minds, but with all our heart and with all our soul and with all our mind. And if we leave any part out, then we are falling short in our worship. We are to honor God with all of our emotions. Even with our anger.

Paul says, *"Be angry..."* What does he mean? I want to suggest that this is not a command to be angry. The Greek text can be translated either as a command or as a statement of being:

- Be angry!
- You are angry.

For this reason, the NIV has translated this, *"In your anger, do not sin."* There are also times when anger is inappropriate. There is a keen distinction here. Paul has ordered us to "speak the truth in love." It is possible to speak the truth, but not to do it in love. Speaking the truth with any other mode than love is a violation of this command. Likewise, there are times when I should be angry. But there are also times when I should recognize that my anger is misdirected.

1. We are not to be bad-tempered people.

    When we get to verse 31 Paul tells us to put away all *"bitterness and wrath and anger and clamor..."* While anger is not in itself sinful, that is not where the Christian is to live. While anger is not in itself sinful, it can often lead to sin.

2. One of the qualifications for an elder is that he is not to be quick-tempered (Titus 1:7), but rather, he is to be gentle and uncontentious (I Timothy 3:3).

3. We are not to be easily provoked. I Corinthians 13 says that love is not provoked (13:5). When I am being easily provoked to anger, I am

not showing love. What provokes you to anger? What is it that really gets under your skin and makes your blood boil? Things in your home... community... church? Ask the Lord for the love which enables to bear all things.

Paul goes on to warn that we should *not give the devil an opportunity. (Ephesians 4:25-27)*. Nothing opens the door to Satan as much as losing your temper. The moment you are controlled by your anger, you are no longer being yielded to the Holy Spirit.

This is graphically illustrated in the case of Cain and Abel. You remember the story. It is set in the context of worship. The two brothers had each come to worship the Lord. They each brought the fruit of their labors to sacrifice before the Lord.

- Because he was a keeper of flocks, Abel brought a lamb to sacrifice to the Lord.
- Because he was a farmer, Cain brought an offering of the fruit of the ground.

In some way in which we are not told, it was made known that the Lord honored Abel's offering and did not honor Cain's offering. Why? I'm not really sure. I suspect that this account underscores the importance of a blood sacrifice. Or perhaps the Lord was looking at the heart and the spirit of the worship of the two brothers and found something wanting in Cain. In any case, the offering of Cain was rejected.

What was the result? Cain became angry. He didn't just become angry. He became very angry.

> *...So Cain became very angry and his countenance fell. 6 Then the Lord said to Cain, "Why are you angry? And why has your countenance fallen? 7 If you do well, will not your countenance be lifted up? And if you do not do well, sin is crouching at the door; and its desire is for you, but you must master it." (Genesis 4:5b-7).*

The path of anger can lead to sin. It gathers its companions of bitterness and resentment. And it grows into a wild beast which crouches at the door, ready to pounce.

Two doors. The first is marked "anger." Behind it lies the evil beast of sin, waiting to pounce and devour. It is a door which leads to death and destruction. But there is a second door. Jesus says, *"I stand at the door and knock; if anyone hears My voice and opens the door, I will come in to him, and will dine with him, and he with Me"* (Revelation 3:20). Indeed, He not only stands at the door – He is the door. Through Him we enter into life and peace.

Is there is an uninvited guest in your life? Are you wrestling with old unresolved anger? It smolders below the surface, needing only a casual stirring to spring to full flame. What to do? Deny it? Pretend it isn't there? Ignore it? Jesus gave quite a different approach.

> *"If therefore you are presenting your offering at the altar, and there remember that your brother has something against you, 24 leave your offering there before the altar, and go your way; first be reconciled to your brother, and then come and present your offering." (Matthew 5:23-24).*

Imagine it. You are in the temple. You have advanced to the altar. You are in the midst of worshiping God. But suddenly you remember! There is that old unresolved anger. Leave your worship. Leave your gift. Go and take part in true religion.

The King was preparing for a journey to a far country. He called his servants to him and entrusted them with the care of the land. They were charged with protecting and preserving the inheritance.

Years passed and the King did not return. But he sent messengers to assure the people of their King's love and receive news of the kingdom. The messengers were not well received. One was beaten. Another was murdered. A third was publicly humiliated.

The King was troubled when he heard of the reception which his servants had received. But instead of anger, he responded in love. He called his Son to him and said, "Son, I will send you as the sign of my love. When they see you, they will know that I love them and forgive them." And so, the Son came to the kingdom.

But when the unfaithful servants saw the Son coming, they plotted against him. They said among themselves, "This is the Son - if we kill him, then the inheritance will be ours." And so, they took the Son, scorned him, beat him, and killed him. What is the response of the King? The law of the King demands death. The anger of the King demands vengeance. But the King says...

> "I extend to you my love and my forgiveness.
> "Because my law demands death, let the death of my Son be reckoned as that which paid the penalty for your rebellion.
> "The inheritance which you sought to steal from me, I freely give to you.
> "I declare you to be children of the King."

Someone has said that you can only love if you have been loved and then you will only love to the extent that you have been loved. In the same way, you can only forgive if you have been forgiven and then you will only forgive to the extent that you have been forgiven. The good news is that God's forgiveness is without measure.

There may be times when you do not agree with another Christian brother. There may be differences of opinion. That is alright. There may be strong emotion. That is okay, too. But let us remember that there is One who had every right to be angry with us. Once upon a tree, the anger of God which should have been directed at us was replaced by love. We are charged with doing the same.

YOU ARE WARNED AGAINST STEALING

> *He who steals must steal no longer; but rather he must labor, performing with his own hands what is good, so that he will have something to share with one who has need. (Ephesians 4:28).*

Exodus 20:15 lists the eight commandment as a prohibition against stealing. But instead of merely repeating that command, Paul takes it, makes it personal, and then extends it into a positive statement of Christian giving. He begins by saying that Christians *must steal no longer*. Worded this way, we are led to assume that we have been guilty of stealing in the past. The truth of the matter is that we are all guilty in one way or

> "He who steals" is ὁ κλέπτων (*ho klepton*) from which we get our modern word "kleptomaniac."

another of stealing. It might have been a large theft or it might have been something we deemed inconsequential, but it was nevertheless a theft. It might have been an overt act of taking something that did not belong to us or it might have involved the withholding of that which was justly due.

Paul's injunction is more than merely a prohibition against stealing. He calls for the believer, not merely to abstain from sin, but to be a positive force for good in the world. He is to do this by engaging in work that has as its end result the sharing of goods with those in need. The opposite of stealing is not merely the cessation of thievery; the opposite of stealing is sharing.

What You Were	What You Are to Be
You stole so that you might meet your own desires.	You are to labor so as to be able to share with others.
Your actions resulted in people being in need.	You are to meet the needs of those who have nothing.

Notice that, for the Christian, work is not merely designed for you to be able to meet your own needs without having to steal from others. Work for the Christian is to be a means of serving others. This is true both of the work that you do as well as of the money you are paid for such work. When you work, your labor provides either goods or services that are needed by others. That is why you are paid for your labors. But such pay is not to be an end unto itself. The Christian is to see work as a divine calling. We work in order to serve. We are to labor in order to give to others.

Negative	Neutral	Positive
Steals from others	Does not steal	Works to give to those who are in need

Christianity calls for an exact reversal of lifestyle. The one who once stole is to become a hard worker so that he can taken a portion of his earnings and give to others who are in need. His relationship with Christ has turned him from a taker into a giver.

YOU ARE WARNED AGAINST IMPROPER

SPEECH

> *Let no unwholesome word proceed from your mouth, but only such a word as is good for edification according to the need of the moment, so that it will give grace to those who hear. (Ephesians 4:29).*

We have already seen a reference in verse 25 to the importance of telling the truth. Now we see that, in addition to telling the truth, we are to direct our words for the purpose of edification. It is not enough merely to speak truly. We must also speak in a way that builds up others.

Negative	Neutral	Positive
Unwholesome words coming from your mouth.	Does not say anything	Speaking words of edification that give grace to those who hear.

The reference to an "unwholesome word" is λόγος σαπρὸς (*logos sapros*) and refers to a "rotten word." It is graphic imagery to refer to graphic language. This same word for rottenness is used several times in the gospels to describe rotten fruit (Matthew 7:17-18; 12:33; 13:48; Luke 6:43). This suggests several corollaries between rotten fruit and rotten words.

1. Unwholesome words leave a nasty taste. If you have had the experience of biting into a piece of rotten fruit, you know there are few things that can more easily turn your stomach and take away your appetite. In a similar way, unwholesome words tend to detract any desire for others to listen for the purposes of edification.

2. Unwholesome words can lead to ill spiritual health. In the same way that eating rotten fruit can make you sick, listening to rotten teaching or to evil audible influences can act as a spiritual contagion.

3. Unwholesome words come from a correspondingly bad source. Jesus said *there is no good tree which produces bad fruit, nor, on the other hand, a bad tree which produces good fruit (Luke 6:43).* Unwholesome words reflect a diseased spirit and it is possible to do a diagnosis of a person's soul by listening to the words he speaks.

We are to stop the flow of unwholesome words from our mouth. Yet this is not only a prohibition against engagement in profanity or crude language. It is a call to speak words that build up instead of those that tear down. Our speech is to be dedicated to God. As God is the Creator of heaven and earth, so we are to build up others with our words. As He spoke things into existence and then was able to look back and see that it was all good, so we are to speak good things.

YOU ARE WARNED AGAINST GRIEVING THE SPIRIT

> *Do not grieve the Holy Spirit of God, by whom you were sealed for the day of redemption. (Ephesians 4:30).*

The translators left off the opening word καὶ (*kai*), "and," that shows the connection with the previous verse. This suggests at least one of the ways of grieving the Spirit is by the use of the rotten speech that was described in verse 29. At the same time, we should note that the idea of grieving the Holy Spirit of God is an Old Testament concept. Isaiah speaks of how the Israelites rebelled and grieved the Lord's Holy Spirit.

> *For He said, "Surely, they are My people,*
> *Sons who will not deal falsely."*
> *So He became their Savior.*
> *9 In all their affliction He was afflicted,*
> *And the angel of His presence saved them;*
> *In His love and in His mercy He redeemed them,*
> *And He lifted them and carried them all the days of old.*
> *10 But they rebelled*
> *And grieved His Holy Spirit;*
> *Therefore He turned Himself to become their enemy,*
> *He fought against them. (Isaiah 63:8-10).*

Notice that grieving the Spirit of God resulted in the Lord turning from being a friend to Israel to being their enemy as He now fought against them. Seen in this context, we can begin to understand that it is a dangerous thing to grieve the Spirit of God. It is dangerous to grieve the Spirit because it is the Spirit who has sealed you for the day of redemption.

Paul has already made mention of the fact that we were sealed with the Holy

Spirit of promise (Ephesians 1:13). We noted in our examination of that passage the idea of a seal; that it serves both to protect, to identify ownership, to provide authentication, and to guarantee a promise. It is this last concept that is in view here. We were sealed for the day of redemption and the presence of the Holy Spirit is a guarantee that our redemption will be completed on that day.

What is the day of redemption? It is a reference to that which shall take place when Christ returns. We have been redeemed through faith in Christ, but our redemption is not yet complete. We still await the physical manifestations of that redemption. Today we still struggle with illness and disease, but there is coming a day in the future when these things shall be no more. Paul says in Romans 8:23 that we eagerly await the redemption of our body.

YOU ARE WARNED AGAINST BITTERNESS

Let all bitterness and wrath and anger and clamor and slander be put away from you, along with all malice. 32 *Be kind to one another, tender-hearted, forgiving each other, just as God in Christ also has forgiven you. (Ephesians 4:31-32).*

These last two verses form a unit. Verse 31 presents the negative; verse 32 presents the positive. Verse 31 tells us what we are to remove from our lives; verse 32 tells us what we are to emulate in our lives.

- Bitterness: *Pikria* (πικρία). This is a common theme in the Old Testament where bitterness is often associated with poison. There is something poisonous about bitterness; it eats away at the soul.

- Wrath: *Thumos* (θυμός). This is speaking of the ungodly wrath into which we so commonly fall. On the other hand, Revelation 15:1 can speak of the wrath of God (ὁ θυμὸς τοῦ θεοῦ). The difference is that God's wrath is pure and holy and untainted by sin.

- Anger: *Orge* (ὀργή). This is the more common word for "anger." Wrath and anger are often seen as parallel synonyms in the Old Testament. The Septuagint regularly describes "burning anger" as ὀργὴ θυμοῦ.

- Clamor: *Krauge* (κραυγή). In the context of these other descriptions, this is to be seen as a clamor for the cause of evil.

- Slander: *Blasphemia* (βλασφημία). It is from this word that we derive our modern term "blasphemy." To blaspheme is to speak evil of someone. When we refer to blasphemy, we are describing the act of speaking evil against God. While it is true that we are not to speak evil of God, we are also not to speak evil of people in general.

- Malice: *Kakia* (κακία). This is the simple Greek word for "evil" as opposed to *kalos* (καλος), the word for "good."

The fact that we are given all of these commands tells us something about the Christian life. It tells us that obedience does not come automatically. It tells us there is effort involved in living the Christian life. This is not to deny the work of God in our sanctification, but it is a synergistic work in which the Christian participates. There are things as a Christian you are commanded to do.

At the same time, the Christian is empowered to live the Christian life. The power to live that life is seen in the closing words of this chapter. It is seen in the gospel where *God in Christ also has forgiven you*. This provides both the motivation and the means to living Christianly.

We are motivated to live the Christian life because there is One who lived and who died on our behalf. We tell the truth because He is the truth and spoke truly to us. We release our anger because He satisfied the anger of God against us. We stop stealing and we give to other because He first gave to us. We seek to edify with our words because He is building us up into the very temple of God. We forgive others because we have been forgiven.

The gospel is also the means by which we live the Christian life. It is as I trust in that which God has freely provided that I am changed from the inside out. In the same way I once trusted in Christ for my justification, so now I also am able to trust Him for my sanctification.

CLEAN LIVING IN AN UNCLEAN WORLD
Ephesians 5:1-14

When I was a lot younger, I attended and eventually graduated from what was in that day a world renown Bible college. It was a wonderful experience to be immersed in the study of the Scriptures and the rub shoulders on a daily basis with others who loved the Lord and who were seeking to serve Him. But looking back on those years, I can now see there was something just a bit artificial about that environment. I was living with a Christian roommate, sitting in a Christian classroom, eating in a Christian cafeteria, and reading in a Christian library. It was relatively easy to live at least the semblance of a Christian life because there were not a lot of non-Christian influences I was experiencing.

Paul's epistle to the Ephesians is written to a people who were living in the real world. Ephesus was a pagan city with pagan ideals and a pagan lifestyle. There were the ancient version of billboards advertizing sex, sin, and sacrilege. The temptation to return to that sort of lifestyle would have been a daily experience. It is in this context that Paul issues his call for Christians to clean living in a dirty world.

FRAGRANT IMITATIONS

> *Therefore be imitators of God, as beloved children; 2 and walk in love, just as Christ also loved you and gave Himself up for us, an offering and a sacrifice to God as a fragrant aroma. (Ephesians 5:1-2).*

This section begins with the word "therefore" and thus connects to the previous chapter. Paul closed verse 31 with a call for believers to *be kind to one another, tender-hearted, forgiving each other, just as God in Christ also has forgiven you.* Because God in Christ has forgiven you, you are to be imitators of God, demonstrating that same forgiveness toward others as you walk in love toward them.

The word "imitator" is translated from the Greek *mimetes* (μιμητής). It is from this same Greek word that we derive our English term "mimic." We are to imitate God. Notice that this imitation is to be done *as beloved children*. There is something about a child that leads him to naturally imitate his parents. I am certain that you have seen a child try to walk around the house while wearing mom or dad's shoes. It is natural that children try to emulate their parents.

When we seek to emulate our parents, we are seeking to follow a pattern that may have both positive and negative qualities. That is because they are fallen creatures who have been tainted by sin. But when we seek to imitate God, we are following the perfect pattern; the One who is holy and without sin.

There are two commands given in these two verses and they are given in parallel:

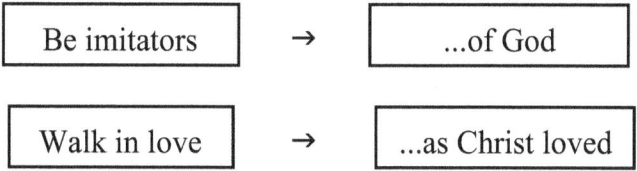

Here is the point. If you are walking in love as Christ first loved us, then you are being an imitator of God. The opposite is also true; if you are imitating God, then you will be reflecting the love of Christ. You cannot say that you are following Christ if you are not also showing love to others.

The love of Christ that was demonstrated on the cross is described by Paul as a fragrant aroma. John MacArthur makes this observation:

> While Christ was the sin-bearer, God could not look on Him or rejoice in Him or be pleased in Him. But when the Father raised Christ from the dead, the sacrifice that caused Him to become sin became the sacrifice that conquered sin. The sin that put Him to death was itself put to death, and that great act of love was to God as a fragrant aroma. That fragrant aroma spreads its fragrance to everyone on earth who will place himself under the grace of that sacrifice, and it will spread its fragrance throughout heaven for all eternity (186:199).

When we reflect the love of Christ, imitating God as we show love for others, the result is that we also spread that same fragrance in our world. When our Christian lives exhibit a sweet smell, the result is that others will be attracted to Christ. The corollary of this is when there is a stench to our Christian lives others will be repulsed by the message we claim to represent.

SIGNIFICANT SPEECH

> *But immorality or any impurity or greed must not even be named among you, as is proper among saints; 4 and there must be no filthiness and silly talk, or coarse jesting, which are not fitting, but rather giving of thanks. (Ephesians 5:3-4).*

There is a little nursery rhyme that says, "Sticks and stones may break my bones, but words will never hurt me." It isn't true. Our words are terribly important and can have severe repercussions.

Paul begins by citing three things that are not even to be named among believers. If these things are not to be even named by believers, then it should go without saying that believers should not engage in outward engagement and participation of these same activities.

- Immorality.
- Impurity.
- Greed.

Not only are we to abstain from participating in these sins, we are not even to entertain them in our speech. It is along these same lines that Paul goes on to say that we should abstain from *filthiness and silly talk, or coarse jesting.* Such speech is inappropriate for the child of God. Instead of cursing or coarse language, our tongues should be engaged in that which honors God.

We live in a day and an age where such language is commonplace. You can hardly turn on a television or walk down a supermarket isle or enter the workplace without being confronted with such occurrences of profanity and improper speech. As you regularly hear such language, it filters into your subconscious and it is not long before you are being tempted to think such thoughts and speak in a similar way. How can you fight such influences? I would suggest that it is by mentally confronting them each and every time they come into the range of your hearing. As you hear such language, hold a conversation with the Lord, giving thanks for the purity to which He has

DISOBEDIENT DETRACTORS

For this you know with certainty, that no immoral or impure person or covetous man, who is an idolater, has an inheritance in the kingdom of Christ and God. 6 Let no one deceive you with empty words, for because of these things the wrath of God comes upon the sons of disobedience. (Ephesians 5:5-6).

The reason we are to avoid even speaking of immorality and impurity and that which generates covetousness is because these things are not a part of our future inheritance. Indeed, these qualities make one ineligible for the kingdom of God. Instead, they make one eligible for the wrath of God.

Paul was not telling the Ephesians anything they did not already know. He indicates they already have a certainty about such things. They had an awareness that God is without sin and that He will not abide with that which is sinful.

At the same time, the Ephesians lived in a city that was known for its pagan influences. The city was home to the Temple of Artemis, the Greek hunter-goddess of fertility. She was regularly portrayed in the temple with a plethora of breasts, a picture of great fertility. As went the religion, so also went the lifestyle. Both the Greeks and the Romans considered themselves to be moral, but their brand of morality

Artemis, in the Ephesus Museum

thought nothing of sexual experiences outside the bounds of marriage and even less regarding humor aimed at such experiences. In one of his speeches, Cicero describes the typical Roman view of sexual morality:

> By general consent we concede a young man a few wild oats. Nature herself showers adolescence with a veritable spate of desires; if the dam bursts without endangering anyone's life or breaking up anyone's home, we put up with it easily and cheerfully. (Cicero: Pro Caelio).

Within the Greek culture, it was considered commonplace for a man engage in sexual relations with a young boy, with a slave, or with a social inferior. Slaves of both genders were regularly forced into such relationships. Barclay sums up the attitudes of the pagan culture of that day: "It has been said that chastity was the one new virtue which Christianity introduced into the world. It is certainly true that the ancient world regarded sexual immorality so lightly that it was no sin at all" (1976:161).

There is a deception against which Paul warns and it is just as relevant in today's culture as it was in the day of the New Testament. The "empty words" of this deception state that God is not concerned about such issues as sexuality, morality, or purity. Today's culture calls for people to engage in whatever action they wish. But just as adults are careful lest their children partake of that which is physically harmful to themselves, so God warns us of that which brings the worst possible calamity into our lives.

DEPARTING FROM DARKNESS

> *Therefore do not be partakers with them; 8 for you were formerly darkness, but now you are Light in the Lord; walk as children of Light 9 (for the fruit of the Light consists in all goodness and righteousness and truth), 10 trying to learn what is pleasing to the Lord. 11 Do not participate in the unfruitful deeds of darkness, but instead even expose them; 12 for it is disgraceful even to speak of the things which are done by them in secret. (Ephesians 5:7-12).*

Paul calls for his readers to live differently because they have been saved from that previous lifestyle. Note the contrast between these two realms:

What You Were	What You Have Become
Darkness.	Light in the Lord.
Practiced the unfruitful deeds of darkness.	The fruit of the light consists in all goodness, righteousness, and truth.

It is not merely that we used to walk in darkness and are now to walk in the light. It is that you were darkness. The quality of darkness identified who you were. Now you have a new identity; it is in the Lord. Paul says that you are light. But it is not an independent light. You are light in the Lord. As you are in Christ, so you are in the light and you are considered to be light. Because of that new identification, you are now to walk as children of light.

Do not miss this connection. This is not the way of religion that says, "Do good in order to be accepted by God." Instead, this is the way of grace that says, "You have been made to be light in the Lord, now walk in that light." Here is the point: the root is evidenced by the fruit. What you do is a result of what you are. The Lord says, "I have made you into someone different; now be that person."

LIVING IN THE LIGHT

> *But all things become visible when they are exposed by the light, for everything that becomes visible is light. 14 For this reason it says, "Awake, sleeper, and arise from the dead, and Christ will shine on you." (Ephesians 5:13-14).*

Having been married for more than 35 years and having raised a daughter who is now grown with children of her own, I have noticed that when women apply their makeup, they normally do it before a mirror and under several bright lights. Why? It is so they can see any defects and correct them. Light helps you to see where the problems are located.

Because you are in the light and because light exposes all things for what they are, you are to live in a wakeful way. What does that mean? It means you are to live intentionally, not as though you were still in the deadness of your sin or the darkness of

> Paul is quoting from Isaiah 26:19 and 60:1. There are some who think these verses were placed together in an early baptismal liturgy.

your previously lost condition. It means you are to let the light of Christ shine upon you, practicing the presence of the Savior. How would you act if you knew Jesus were watching? The point is that He is watching.

WALKING IN SUBMISSION
Ephesians 5:15-21

Ever since we passed Ephesians 4:1, we have been seeing an ongoing theme. It is expressed in the single word "walk." Paul has been telling us how we ought to walk in our Christian life.

- Therefore I, the prisoner of the Lord, implore you to walk in a manner worthy of the calling with which you have been called (Ephesians 4:1).
- So this I say, and affirm together with the Lord, that you walk no longer just as the Gentiles also walk, in the futility of their mind (Ephesians 4:17).
- Therefore be imitators of God, as beloved children; 2 and walk in love, just as Christ also loved you and gave Himself up for us (Ephesians 5:1-2).
- You were formerly darkness, but now you are Light in the Lord; walk as children of Light (Ephesians 5:8).

As we come to verse 15 of the fifth chapter, the same theme continues. Indeed, the passage begins with a call to be careful how you walk. By now it is quite obvious that Paul uses walking as a metaphor for living. Everyone lives. You are always moving toward God or you are moving away from Him. The one thing you are never doing is standing still. The question is whether you are living wisely or foolishly.

THE WAY OF WISE WALKING

> *Therefore be careful how you walk, not as unwise men but as wise, 16 making the most of your time, because the days are evil. 17 So then do not be foolish, but understand what the will of the Lord is. (Ephesians 5:15-17).*

When you think of wisdom in the Bible, you probably think first and foremost of the book of Proverbs. It is a book that is all about wisdom. It teaches the reader about the skill of living. But Proverbs is not the only place where wisdom is found in the Bible. Paul is going to give us a series of lessons on this same skill of living. Just as the Proverbs begin by telling us of the importance of wisdom before taking us

> This passage begins with the word "therefore," indicating a conclusion based on what has been said previously. In verse 14, Paul used two Old Testament texts to call his readers to wake up so that Christ could shine on them. Now that they are awake, they are to walk in a careful manner.

to the individual application of that wisdom, so Paul also begins this section with some general lessons of wisdom before taking us to some very specific applications.

1. Wise Walking Takes Effort: *Therefore be careful how you walk, not as unwise men but as wise (5:15).*

    It doesn't take any effort at all to walk foolishly. All you have to do is move. But it takes real care to walk in wisdom. The Greek phrasing is literally, "See that you walk accurately, not as unwise, but as wise."

    It is important to walk carefully because there are hidden dangers. A friend of mine who worked in the fire department responded one night to a situation on board a barge. The deck was dark and my friend had no flashlight. As he walked across the deck, he was unaware that a portion of the deck plating had been removed by crew members making repairs. He stepped into a jagged opening, fell, and tore his leg wide open on the sharp metal. It was an important lesson in walking carefully.

    The Greeks prided themselves for their wisdom. But it was not a wisdom that actually made you live better. It was a wisdom that questioned everything and that produced endless discussions, but which had little in the way of a positive outcome. By contrast, the wisdom of God teaches you how to live.

2. Wise Walking Involves Planning and Deliberation: *Making the most of your time, because the days are evil (5:16).*

    The King James Version is a more literal translation when it reads, "Redeeming the time" (ἐξαγοραζόμενοι τὸν καιρόν). A similar use of ἐξαγοραζω (*exagorazo*) is used in the Septuagint, the Greek translation of Daniel 2:8 where the king accuses his servants of "bargaining for time."

We have been redeemed and that placed us into the redemption business. We are called to redeem out time, to make it count for the purposes for which we were redeemed. What is it that wastes time in your life? Perhaps that is an area of your life that has not been redeemed.

I am not saying we must become workaholics. If we look at the example of Jesus, we see someone who regularly took time off from ministry to go and spend quiet time with the Lord. He knew how to work and He knew how to rest and He knew how to redeem the time. The reason Paul gives for the importance of redeeming the time is because the days are evil. There is evil at work and it will succeed unless we redeem the time.

3. Wise Walking Invokes the Will of the Lord: *So then do not be foolish, but understand what the will of the Lord is (5:17).*

How can we determine what the will of the Lord is? One of the questions I am regularly asked concerns the will of the Lord. When the Bible uses the term, it can mean one of two things:

- Everything that happens in history is the will of the Lord: Paul has already said in this epistle that God works all things after the council of his own will. This is speaking of God's eternal plan for the ages in which He not only knows the future, but is working to bring about all that shall take place.

- His will is comprised of His revealed commands. When God tells us to do something, we can say that He is revealing His will to us. I believe this to be the meaning here. We are to work to know what God wants from us; to determine what He has told us to do, and then we are to do it.

Our problem is that we get sidetracked into doing other things. It is not only that we fall into sin; it is also that we fall into doing things that do not necessarily need to be done in the first place. The author of the epistle to the Hebrews calls for his readers to lay aside sin, but he also calls for them to lay aside every weight (Hebrews 12:1-2). Some things weigh us down that are not in themselves wrong. But they should still be discarded if they hinder us from doing the will of God.

THE SPIRIT-FILLED LIFE

And do not get drunk with wine, for that is dissipation, but be filled with the Spirit, 19 speaking to one another in psalms and hymns and spiritual songs, singing and making melody with your heart to the Lord; 20 always giving thanks for all things in the name of our Lord Jesus Christ to God, even the Father; 21 and be subject to one another in the fear of Christ. (Ephesians 5:18-21).

Paul begins this section with a negative and a positive command. We are meant to see them in contrast to one another:

What you are not to do	What you are to do
Be drunk with wine	Be filled with the Spirit

The negative command involves drinking and drunkenness: *do not get drunk with wine (5:18).* The Bible never commands a complete abstinence from alcoholic beverage, except for those instances under the Old Covenant when someone had taken a special vow to that effect. On the other hand, the Bible always condemns drunkenness.

Of course, there are some people who have a predisposition for drunkenness and a weakness in the area of alcoholism. It is better for such people not to drink at all. Likewise, there is always a danger that someone can begin to drink as a result of social peer pressure. Such dangers ought not to be ignored.

Stott makes four simple observations from the Greek text of this command to *be filled with the Spirit*:

- It is in the imperative mood. This is the mood of command. It is a call to action. We are called to accomplish that which will result in the filling of the Spirit.

- It is in the plural form. Those from the southern states would translate this to say, "Ya'll be filled with the Spirit." It is a call and a command that goes to the entire church of Ephesus, not merely to its elders and deacons. It is a call and a command that goes to every believer in the church today.

- It is in the passive voice. Even though it is given in the imperative as something in which you are involved as to its execution, the command itself is passive. You cannot fill yourself with the Spirit. It is the Spirit that must fill you. How can you accomplish such a thing? It is by yielding your life to His influence. In the same way that one comes under the influence of alcoholic beverages, so you are called to come under the influence of the Spirit.

What does it mean to be filled with the Spirit? One way of answering this question is to ask what it means to be filled with wine. When you are filled with wine, you come under its influence. It takes over and you find yourself doing and saying things you would not normally do or say. The filling of the Spirit is like that. When you come under the influence of the Spirit, you do and say things that are in accordance with the Spirit.

- It is in the present tense. When a command is given in the present tense in the Greek language, it carries the idea of a continuity of action. This means you are to be continually filled with the Spirit.

What follows this initial command are a series of present participles (*speaking, singing, making melody, giving thanks, being subject*). Whenever you come across a Greek present participle, the action of that participle is meant to coincide with the action of the main verb (as opposed to the aorist participle in which the action of the participle would precede that of the main verb). In this case, the main verb is seen in the command to "be filled with the Spirit." The actions that are to coincide with that filling is seen in the following statements that further describe the Spirit-filled life.

1. It is to be a Life of Community: *Speaking to one another in psalms and hymns and spiritual songs, singing and making melody with your heart to the Lord (5:19)*.

   There is a focus here upon community. While we are making melody to God, we are also speaking to one another. Our worship is vertical, but there is a horizontal relationship that also takes place amidst that worship of God. John MacArthur makes the following observation regarding music in the church:

> For over a thousand dark years of its history (c:500-1500) the church in general did not sing. From shortly after New Testament times until the Reformation, what music the church had was usually performed by professional musicians. The music they presented could not be understood or appreciated by the average church member. In any case, they could only sit and listen, unable to participate. But when the Bible came back into the church during the Reformation, singing came with it (258).

The music and liturgy of the church is more than a mere religious exercise. These activities are meant to speak to our soul and to breathe faith into us, even as we direct our faith and our hope to the Lord.

2. It is to be a Life of Thanksgiving: *Always giving thanks for all things in the name of our Lord Jesus Christ to God, even the Father (5:20).*

You have heard of the fellow who struggled to have a thankful attitude in spite of the fact that he had no shoes; it changed when he met someone who had no feet.

> Stott points out that "the grumbling spirit is not compatible with the Holy Spirit (1979:207).

The point of the story is that thankfulness comes from perspective. It is when we see our own undeservedness that we can be thankful for that which we have. Then it is as we realize that all good things come from the Lord that we have a direction to our thankfulness.

This is important. Thanksgiving must always have a proper direction if it is to be true thankfulness. We must be thankful to the One who has given us that for which we are thankful. Paul tells us that our thanksgiving is to go through Jesus to God; that is, through the Son to the Father.

3. It is to be a Life of Subjection: *Be subject to one another in the fear of Christ (5:21).*

The Spirit-filled life involves not merely subjection to the influence of the Spirit, but also subjection to one another. We have already noted that there is a focus here on community, but now we see that this is to be a community of those who are serving one another and who are subject to one another. This will be seen in a variety of ways throughout the rest of this chapter:

> The phrase "be subject" in the Greek text is the present participle of ὑποτάσσω (*hupotasso*), "being subject to one another." The word carries the idea of placing one's own desires under another.

- Wives are to be subject to their husbands (5:22-24).
- Husbands are to love their wives as Christ loved the church (5:25-31).
- Children are to be subject to their parents, obeying them and honoring them (6:1-3).
- Fathers are to bring up their children in such a way that does not provoke them to anger (6:4).
- Slaves are to be subject to their masters (6:5-8).
- Masters are to treat slaves in a corresponding attitude of subjection as to the Lord (6:9).

Each of these relationships are to be characterized by a form of subjection. It is not only the slaves who are to be subject to their masters, but their masters are also called to submit their own masterly desires as they give up the masterly right to threaten as they remember that they have their own Master in heaven. Not only are children to obey their parents, but fathers are to obey the Lord and therefore be gentle with their children as they teach them God's ways. Not only are wives to be subject to their husbands, but husbands are to temper their own priorities so that their lives are given over to love their wives.

INSTRUCTIONS TO WIVES
Ephesians 5:22-24

We have already noted how the first half of Paul's epistle to the Ephesians was dedicated to explaining what God has done for us; how He has blessed us with every spiritual blessing and how He has showered us with the riches of His grace. When we came to chapter 4, Paul began to explain how we ought to live as a result of those riches. The instructions that are subsequently given in chapters 4 and 5 of Ephesians are general in nature; they are directed equally to the entire church. Now there is a change. Beginning with this passage, Paul becomes specific as he targets first one group and then another. He begins with wives.

THE CALL TO SUBJECTION

> *Wives, be subject to your own husbands, as to the Lord. (Ephesians 5:22).*

Most people lift this verse out of its context as if it were a stand-alone command. But if you look at it in the Greek text, it is immediately obvious that we cannot do that, for the verb is absent. If you were to give a woodenly literal translation of this verse by itself, it would read, "Wives, to your own husbands, as to the Lord." What happened to the verb? What happened to the subjection? It is found in the previous verse. It is a verse, not merely speaking of women, but to people of all genders. Let's back up a few verses to see the context::

> Do not get drunk with wine
> but
> be filled with the Spirit,
>   speaking to one another...
>   singing and making melody...
>   always giving thanks...
>   being subject to one another in the fear of Christ,
>   wives, to your own husbands.

This means the command for wives to be subject to their own husbands grows out of the previous command for all Christians to be subject to one another. One of the ways in which all Christians are to be subject to one another is that wives are to show that submissive spirit to their own husbands.

Wives are indeed to be in subjection to their husbands. But that is not all. We are all to be in subjection one to another. Children to parents. Slaves to masters. Employees to employers. Citizens to their governments. Church members to their church leaders. The Christian life is a life of submission. Even Christ learned submission and we are to learn it, too.

While it might seem to be a fine line between the two, John MacArthur points out that this is not, strictly speaking, a call to obedience, but a call to subjection:

> The wife is not commanded to obey (*hupakouo*) her husband, as children are to obey their parents and slaves their masters (6:1, 5). A husband is not to treat his wife as a servant or as a child, but as an equal for whom God has given him care and responsibility for provision and protection, to be exercised in love 1986:280-1).

We shall have more to say about husbands and their own role in the marriage as well as the manner in which they are to bring their own priorities and desires into subjection to serve their marriages.

Wives are to be subject to their husbands *as to the Lord*. Notice the point of comparison. They are to be subject to their husbands as though they were being subject to Christ. When we get to verse 25, we shall see a similar point of comparison in the directions given to husbands – they will be told to love their wives *as Christ loved the church*. In both these commands, our attitude toward our spouse is to be changed as a result of our union with Christ.

Our tendency is to retort, "I will be like Christ toward my spouse as long as he/she is correspondingly like Christ toward me." But we are given no assurance that there will be a corresponding movement on the part of our spouse. Instead, the Christian is called to be like Christ no matter whether or not the same attitude is reflected from the spouse. After all, Christ loved us and gave Himself for us when we were His enemies (Romans 5:10).

THE REASON FOR THE CALL

> *For the husband is the head of the wife, as Christ also is the head of the church, He Himself being the Savior of the body. (Ephesians 5:23).*

The reason wives are called to be subject to their husbands is because the Lord has designed marriage to be reflective of His relationship with the church. The husband is the head of the wife as Christ is the head of the church.

The Husband	...is the head of...	The Wife
Christ	...is the head of...	The Church

This position of headship is one that goes all the way back to the Garden of Eden. Adam was created first; then Eve. Before there was ever a fall and before the role of men and women were affected by sin, the principle of the headship of the husband was established. It was a creation ordinance.

It is true that this role has often been accompanied throughout history by harshness and injustice and a lack of love. Sin has taken what was designed to be loving and supportive and has often turned it into something more akin to slavery and brutality, but that does not mean there is something wrong with the roles that were established at creation.

When Paul speaks of Christ *Himself being the Savior of the body*, this is a reminder that Jesus Himself learned submission when He was obedient to the point of going to the cross. He is our pattern and He does not call us to do anything that He has not first done for us.

THE PATTERN OF THE CALL

> *But as the church is subject to Christ, so also the wives ought to be to their husbands in everything. (Ephesians 5:24).*

In setting forth the pattern of submission, Paul now repeats his earlier injunction. Instead of speaking of headship, he now underscores the resulting subjection that is to take place.

| The Church | ...is subject to... | Christ |

| Wives | ...to their... | Husbands |

Once again, Paul does not include the word "subject" in the actual command and it must be understood from the previous phrase. The point its that wives are to stand in relation to their husbands as the church stands in relation to Christ. Paul adds that this is to take place *in everything*. While our modern tendency is to minimize this command, Paul maximizes it.

At the same time, we should add that other Scriptures would indicate there are some limits to such subjection. Just as we are elsewhere instructed by Paul to be subject to governing authorities, that does not mean we are to obey those authorities when they instruct us to do something that is contrary to the Word of God. If a government tells us to abandon our faith in God, we are to listen to God rather than to men in that specific area. The apostles give us the example for such civil disobedience when, in the days of the early church, they were commanded by the civil authorities to stop preaching the name of Christ. They refused and they suffered the consequences.

Finally, it should be pointed out that Paul does not say it is the husband's responsibility to make certain that his wife submits. He will be given his responsibilities in the next paragraph – it will be to love his wife and Christ loved the church. The wife is told to submit to her husband as she would submit to Christ.

We are to treat others as we want to treat Christ. This idea is found throughout the New Testament. Jesus spoke about treating the poor and the needy as though they were Christ. He said in Matthew 25:40 that as you treat those in need, so you are doing it to Him. Wives are told the same thing; as you treat your husband, so you are treating your Lord and Savior, Jesus Christ.

INSTRUCTIONS TO HUSBANDS
Ephesians 5:25-33

The previous section focused on instructions to wives. Now we move to the husbands as they are also given instructions. It must be remembered that all of these instructions stem from the original command that believers are to be submissive to one another. We saw in the previous section that this related to wives and how they were to be submissive to their own husbands. Now we see that same mutual submission is directed toward husbands as they submit by loving their wives as Christ loved the church. This section will be presented in four parts:

5:25-27	5:28-30	5:30-32	5:33
What Christ has done in loving the church	How husbands are to treat their wives: as their own bodies	The union between husbands and wives, Christ and the church	Summary instructions
Loving as Christ loved	Loving your own body	Loving and joining	Loving and respecting

In hearing these instructions, we must keep in mind how extraordinary they would sound to the ancient reader. Klyne Snodgrass helps to put this passage into its historical perspective:

> "In a few places like Sparta and Egypt women were given greater freedom and responsibility. In most places, however, if they were allowed to live at birth, women were minimally educated, could not be witnesses in a court of law, could not adopt children or make a contract, could not own property or inherit, and were viewed, as both Aristotle and Josephus said, in all respects to be inferior to a man. They were seen as less intelligent, less moral, the source of sin, and a continual temptation (see Ecclesiasticus 25:13 - 26:27)"

(1996:303).

Paul's instructions to men were to do that which went against the culture and custom of the day. They were to act in a way that was contrary to the social norms. Their pattern was that which had been established by Christ Himself.

LOVING AS CHRIST LOVED

Husbands, love your wives, just as Christ also loved the church and gave Himself up for her, 26 so that He might sanctify her, having cleansed her by the washing of water with the word, 27 that He might present to Himself the church in all her glory, having no spot or wrinkle or any such thing; but that she would be holy and blameless. (Ephesians 5:25-27).

This section begins with a call for husbands to love their wives. Nothing is said about generating a feeling or an emotion. Too often, we hear in our culture of those who have "fallen in love" or who have "fallen out of love." Such language is foreign to this passage as it is foreign to Scripture. We are called to be in control of our affections. How does one do such a thing?

> Much has been made by Bible teachers over the Greek word for love. It is *agape* and it is the general word for "love."

Harold Hoehner points out how the use of "the present imperative reinforces the idea that a husband's love for his wife is to be an ongoing process. Thus in this context husbands are to love their wives even when they may seem undeserving and unloving, in other words, unconditionally. Its intent is to seek the highest good in the one loved" (2006:747).

It is interesting to note that a later epistle addressed to this same church at Ephesus accused the believers there of having lost their first love. In Revelation 2:5, that church is told to remember their past heritage, to repent of their loveless state, and then to "do the deeds you did at first." They are to remember what it was like to be a loving people and they are to desire to return and then they are to act the way they did when they loved. The same instructions work in a marriage as well as they work in a church. In both cases, our love is to mirror the love of Christ.

1. The Past Work of Christ's Love: *Christ also loved the church and gave Himself up for her (5:25).*

   The love of Christ is seen in the fact that He gave Himself up for the church. He put our welfare before His own. He subjected His own comfort and His own prerogatives in order to serve us.

   Husbands are called to do the same thing. We noted in the previous section how wives are to be subject to their own husbands, but now we find that husbands are to subject themselves on behalf of their own wives as Christ subjected Himself on our behalf.

2. The Present Work of Christ's Love: *So that He might sanctify her, having cleansed her by the washing of water with the word (5:26).*

   Christ is at work today, sanctifying the church. Sanctification is that process by which we are made to be more and more like Christ by means of the work of the Holy Spirit in our lives. That does not mean we sit back and wait for it to happen. It is a process in which we participate. Thus, Philippians 2:12-13 tells us to work out our salvation with fear and trembling and then goes to explain that *it is God who is at work in you, both to will and to work for His good pleasure.*

   Of course, husbands are not able to sanctify or provide spiritual cleansing for their wives, but they can and should serve as spiritual leaders who are seeking to positively influence that sanctification and that cleansing.

   > Stott suggests the reference to "cleansing" might be "a deliberate allusion to the bridal bath which took place before both Jewish and Greek weddings" (1979:227).

   One of the ways in which husbands demonstrate their love for their wives ought to be in the spiritual nurture and cultivation that takes place in their lives. They can and should pray for their wives and with their wives. They should demonstrate a desire for corporate worship and they should make sure they do not become a source for spiritual stumbling on the part of their wives.

   The reference to the "washing of water with the word" calls to mind the ritual of baptism. There is in water baptism the outward sign of washing that represents the inward cleansing that takes place in sanctification. It is a sanctification that takes place "with the word." Instead of λόγος (*logos*), the Greek word here for "word" is ῥῆμα (*rhema*), generally referring to the spoken word. It is as the word is preached and believed that we are cleansed.

3. The Future Work of Christ's Love: *That He might present to Himself the church in all her glory, having no spot or wrinkle or any such thing; but that she would be holy and blameless (5:27).*

The goal of Christ's saving work is that we might come to look like Him, *having no spot or wrinkle or any such thing*, but that we should *be holy and blameless*. He is preparing a spotless bride and one day that work shall be completed.

There is an old saying that goes, "A woman marries a man thinking he will change; a man marries a woman thinking she won't." It underscores the truth that, while we generally do not change a lot on the inside, we do gradually change on the outside. If we live long enough, there will come wrinkles and grey hair and sagging body parts. But if we are being sanctified, there will be a wonderful inward change involving a putting aside of sin and a transformation that makes us more and more like Jesus. If a husband loves his wife as Christ loves the church, then he will look forward with eagerness to see that Christ-like transformation taking place.

LOVING YOUR BODY

> *So husbands ought also to love their own wives as their own bodies. He who loves his own wife loves himself; 29 for no one ever hated his own flesh, but nourishes and cherishes it, just as Christ also does the church, 30 because we are members of His body. (Ephesians 5:28-30).*

Husbands are called to love their wives as they love themselves; to care for their wives as they care for their own bodies. How do you treat your body? You feed it. Perhaps you exercise it. When it is hurting, you do what you can to ease its discomfort. You cannot help but to be aware of its needs and it is only natural to protect it.

Here is the point. When a man loves his wife, he is loving himself because to love her is to love his own flesh. These words take us back to the creation of the woman and the first marriage that was described in terms of a "one flesh" relationship.

> *For this reason a man shall leave his father and his mother, and be joined to his wife; and they shall become one flesh. (Genesis 2:24).*

When a man and woman marry, they cease to be two separate and distinct individuals. There is a joining together that is to continue as long as they both shall live. They become joined together in a manner that is graphically illustrated in the sexual union.

LOVING AND JOINING

> *For this reason a man shall leave his father and mother and shall be joined to his wife, and the two shall become one flesh. 32 This mystery is great; but I am speaking with reference to Christ and the church. (Ephesians 5:31-32).*

Paul now cites an ancient passage. It is taken from the book of Genesis and is the marriage pronouncement of the first marriage. It was ordained that a man would leave his father and mother and be joined to a wife to make a new union. The two would become one, not merely in the sexual union, but in their goals and objectives, in their desires and needs. They would unite in the forming of their marriage.

> One of the obvious implications of this verse is that marriage is to be permanent. This needs to be stressed, not because it is obscure in the text, but because our 21st Century society has so largely ignored this concept.

This contradicted the culture of the Roman world. The Romans were intensely patriarchal in nature. The culture of the day called for a woman to leave her father and her mother and to cleave to her husband. But this passage says something different. It is the man who is to leave father and mother to cleave to his wife.

This is mirrored in what Christ did for us. He is the husband who left His rightful place in heaven to come to the earth and to be identified with His people. He cleaved to His bride in the ultimate sense when He gave Himself up on the cross for her.

Martyn Lloyd-Jones points out the ramifications of this union: "...the whole of the husband's thinking must include his wife also. He must never think of himself in isolation or in detachment. The moment he does so he has broken the most fundamental principle of marriage" (1984:213).

LOVING AND RESPECTING

Nevertheless, each individual among you also is to love his own wife even as himself, and the wife must see to it that she respects her husband. (Ephesians 5:33).

Paul summarizes with what at first seems to be a repetition of the previous commands. Each man is to love his own wife as himself. This has already been thoroughly explained in the preceding verses. The second command is directed toward the wife; she is to respect her husband. The term translated "respect" is the present subjunctive of φοβέω (*phobeo*), literally, "to fear." It is the root from which we derive our term "phobia." Hoehner observes that "in modern times people have a tendency to shy away from the stronger idea of fear. At times, they even have difficulty with the milder concept of respect. However, the philological evidence of this word never carries the idea of 'respect' but always the idea of 'fear'" (2006:783).

At the same time, it must be admitted that the idea is not that the woman is to be terrified of her husband, but rather that she is to treat him with the honor and esteem due his position.

The command for husbands to love their wives is given in the imperative. The corresponding injunction for wives to fear/respect their husbands is addressed as a subjunctive – she should do this. Though it still retains the sense of a command, it is stated in less commanding terms.

Paul has already spoken to the Ephesians about the fear of the Lord they are to express. At the outset of this section, he told the Ephesians to be subject to one another in the fear of Christ (Ephesians 5:21). In the same way, wives are now told to show this same attitude that is due Christ to their husbands. The point in verse 21 was that our fear of Christ should lead us to be subject to one another as we are being subject to Christ. It is in this same way that women are told to be subject to their own husbands.

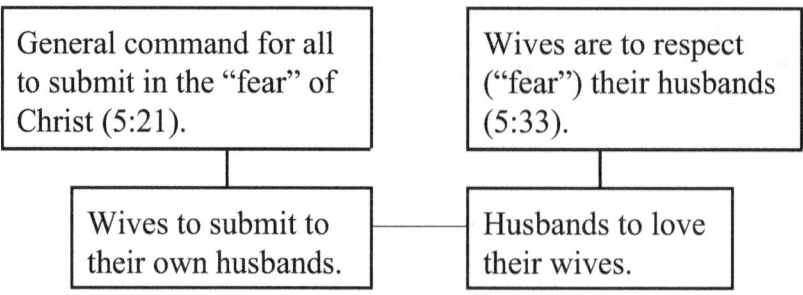

One question that must be asked is why Paul commands women to fear/respect their husbands instead of to love them. When he gives instructions to Titus, he has him instruct the older women to teach the younger women to love their husbands (Titus 2:3-4), but such an injunction is notably absent here. It is perhaps because it is not until a wife comes to respect her husband that she is really able to love him.

INSTRUCTIONS TO CHILDREN AND FATHERS
Ephesians 6:1-4

As our chapter opens, Paul is still dealing with the same general topic that he began in the previous chapter. It is the general topic of relationships. The point has been made that our relationship with Jesus Christ overflows to impact every other relationship. Christian wives are to act differently because of their Christianity; they are to be subject to their husbands in a way that reflects their subjection to Jesus Christ. Christian husbands are to exemplify the very character of Christ by loving their wives as Christ loved the church and gave Himself for it. Now we see this same principle applied to parent-child relationships.

INSTRUCTIONS TO CHILDREN

> *Children, obey your parents in the Lord, for this is right. 2 Honor your father and mother (which is the first commandment with a promise), 3 so that it may be well with you, and that you may live long on the earth. (Ephesians 6:1-3).*

We now move to the commands Paul gives to children. This is a part of the earlier command given by Paul in Ephesians 5:21 to be subject to one another.

> The command for children to obey parents is given as a general blanket statement. The parallel passage in Colossians 3:20 adds that this obedience is to be "in all things."

Wives are to be subject to their husbands, husbands are to subject their love to their wives, and now we find that children are to be subject to their parents. But this time there is a difference. Children are not told merely to be subject to their parents; they are called to obey their parents.

5:22-24	5:25-33	6:1-4
Wives are to be subject to their own husbands	Husbands are to love and care for their wives	Children are to obey their parents

There are several questions that arise as we examine Ephesians 6:1. What qualifies as children? Does this include teenagers? Does it include adult children? The question is by no means a simple one since, under the Roman patriarchal culture, the father had authority over his children as long as he lived, no matter what their age. Indeed, a Roman father could command his married son to divorce his wife and to marry another woman and it was expected to take place.

One obvious departure from the Roman cultural outlook is the command for children to obey both his parents. It does not merely say that the child should obey his father. He is to obey his parents. The parents are mentioned in the plural and therefore include both father and mother.

This same formula was seen in the fifth commandment of the Old Testament law. Paul cites that commandment to *honor your father and mother*. The juxtaposition of these two statements suggest that they are to be seen in parallel with one another.

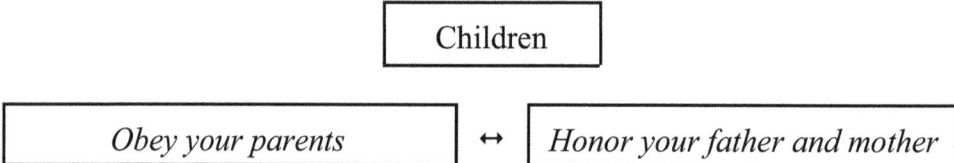

The fact that Paul cites the Mosaic law tells us something about his understanding of the law. He did not see the Ten Commandments as being irrelevant to the Christian life. To the contrary, he cites the law as an authority on how we ought to live. Children are to obey their parents because the law had a corresponding commandment to honor their parents.

What does it mean to honor your parents? The Hebrew text of Exodus 20:12 uses the word kabed (כָּבֵד) to describe this act of honoring parents. It is taken from the same root word that is regularly translated "glory." It literally means "to give weight." The commandment was given in a day before the minting of coins; it was a time when the value of an object was according to its weight.

What does it mean to honor your parents? It means to give weight to who they are and to what they say. It means to value their position. As Paul places this in parallel with the injunction for children to obey their parents, he helps us to understand what it means to honor father and mother.

To honor your parents implies a corresponding obedience. Likewise, the command for children to obey their parents is to be accomplished in a attitude of honor. But that is not all; Paul adds that children are to obey their parents *in the Lord*. The language is similar to what Paul says in Colossians 3:18 when he speaks of wives being subject to their husbands, *as is fitting in the Lord*. The reason children are to obey their parents is because they are in the Lord. This is the way in which people who are in the Lord are called to act.

Some commentators have attempted to limit these instructions only to those cases where there is a Christian home.[1] This is done by taking the phrase "in the Lord" in verse one to refer only to those parents who are "in the Lord." Constance correctly notes that "in the Lord" modifies "obey," not "parents" (2009:67). This is confirmed in Paul's parallel injunction in Colossians 3:20 where he says: *"Children, be obedient to your parents in all things, for this is well-pleasing to the Lord."*

Ephesians 6:1	**Colossians 3:20**
Children, obey your parents in the Lord, for this is right.	*Children, be obedient to your parents in all things, for this is well-pleasing to the Lord.*

Doing something "in the Lord" is a catchphrase that indicates you are doing that action because you are "in Christ" and thus are doing that action for His benefit.

- *Therefore, my beloved brethren, be steadfast, immovable, always abounding in the work of the Lord, knowing that your toil is not in vain **in the Lord*** (1 Corinthians 15:58).
- *Finally, be strong **in the Lord** and in the strength of His might.* (Ephesians 6:10).
- *Receive him then **in the Lord** with all joy, and hold men like him in high regard* (Phiippiansl 2:29).
- *I urge Euodia and I urge Syntyche to live in harmony **in the Lord*** (Philippians 4:2).

This is a command for children to obey their parents as if they were obeying the Lord. Much the same thing will be said in verse 5 to slaves who are to

---

[1] Utley gives such an interpretation (2005:139).

obey their masters as to Christ, that is, as if it were Christ whom they were obeying.

The call is to obey parents as if such a command came from the Lord and because the Christian life is to be lived "in Him." This idea of being "in the Lord" or "in Christ" has pervaded Paul's epistle to the Ephesians. We have noted that it speaks of the position enjoyed by the believer who has been so closely identified with Christ that his very identity is rooted in the person of Jesus.

Because we are in Christ, we are called to live in such a way that reflects that new identity we share with Him. We are called to be obedient in the same way He was obedient. Remember that Hebrews 5:8 says that *He learned obedience from the things which He suffered.* We are similarly called to a life of obedience, not only to the Lord, but to those whom the Lord has placed in authority.

The result of such a life of obedience is a promise: *so that it may be well with you, and that you may live long on the earth.* This is an application of the words of Moses when he said, *"Honor your father and your mother, that your days may be prolonged in the land which the Lord your God gives you" (Exodus 20:12).* This is a significant difference.

The Mosaic Promise	Paul's Application
...that your days may be prolonged in the land which the Lord your God gives you	*...that it may be well with you, and that you may live long on the earth*
This promise had its focus to the promise of the Israelites living in the Promised Land.	This promise is applied more generally to both Jews and Gentiles living on the earth.

Paul sees no problem in taking the promise of a land that was given to the Israelites and applying that to the church composed of both Jews and Gentiles. It is not that the Gentiles are going to inherit a piece of real estate in the eastern Mediterranean, but rather that the covenant relationship they enjoy with God has a similar promise of life and peace in their own lives. When we came to Christ in faith, we entered into a covenant that was promised by the prophets. It is a New Covenant, not written on tablets of stone, but upon the hearts of believers.

This is not to say that every person who obeys his parents is guaranteed to live to be a hundred years old. This is a general rule. It is good and proper and even healthy to listen to your parents.

INSTRUCTIONS TO FATHERS

> *Fathers, do not provoke your children to anger, but bring them up in the discipline and instruction of the Lord. (Ephesians 6:4).*

Now Paul addresses himself to fathers. Whereas the command to children was that they were to obey both their parents, this corresponding command is given only to fathers and not to mothers. This is because fathers were seen as the head of the home in the world of that day. Perhaps it is also because what the mothers do, the fathers are responsible. Fathers may delegate their authority, but they are no less responsible.

This verse contains both a negative as well as a positive command; it tells us what we are not to do and it also tells us what we are to do.

Negative Command	Positive Command
Do not provoke your children to anger	Bring them up in the discipline and instruction of the Lord.

The avoidance of anger in your children does not mean an abstinence of discipline or instruction. To the contrary, fathers are called to bring up their children with a sense of discipline and by giving them godly instruction. On the other hand, this command directs fathers to take the emotional state of their children into consideration when maintaining that discipline and instruction. Discipline should be fair and consistent and seasoned with grace. Our model is our Heavenly Father. His discipline is never unduly harsh and it is often withheld. It is for our benefit and is not given to destroy us.

SLAVES AND MASTERS
Ephesians 6:5-9

Slavery was a way of life in the ancient world. One might become a slave as a result of military conquest, as a punishment for a crime, or because of economic hardship. There were cases in which a person was sold into slavery in order to pay off personal debt. In other cases, a father might have used his children as collateral on a loan which went into default and resulted in the enslavement of those children.

Life as a slave was often quite harsh. In the Roman world, the master had power of life and death over his slave. He could kill his slave on the slightest whim and there would be no legal repercussions. A slave was a commodity to be bought and sold. A slave revolt under Spartacus had taken place a hundred years earlier and it had been ruthlessly put down with the crucifixion of thousands.

The Mosaic Law recognized slavery as an established institution and gave regulations to govern it. Under the law, Jewish slaves were to be set free after six years of servitude (Exodus 21:2). On the other hand, the law allowed a slave to surrender his chance at freedom and to commit himself to a life of slavery (Exodus 21:5-6). This suggests that the lot of the Hebrew slave to a Hebrew master was not quite so fraught with cruelty as it was in the rest of the ancient world.

INSTRUCTIONS TO SLAVES

> *Slaves, be obedient to those who are your masters according to the flesh, with fear and trembling, in the sincerity of your heart, as to Christ; 6 not by way of eyeservice, as men-pleasers, but as slaves of Christ, doing the will of God from the heart. 7 With good will render service, as to the Lord, and not to men, 8 knowing that whatever good thing each one does, this he will receive back from the Lord, whether slave or free. (Ephesians 6:5-8).*

Paul has been dealing with relationships involving authority and submission.

He began back in Ephesians 5:21 with the exhortation for Christians to be submissive to one another in the fear of Christ. He then proceeded to outline some of the practical areas in which such submission was to take place.

...be subject to one another in the fear of Christ (Ephesians 5:21)		
Ephesians 5:21-33	Ephesians 6:1-4	Ephesians 6:5-9
Wives, be subject to your own husbands	Children, obey your parents	Slaves, be obedient to your masters
Husbands, love your wives	Fathers, do not provoke your children	Masters, do the same things to them

In each case, the one who is in the position of submission is first addressed and this is followed with instructions to the one who holds the position of authority. It is interesting to note that Aristotle's Politics makes mention of these same three arenas of relationship when he describes the elemental family relationship as consisting in "master and slave, husband and wife, father and children" (Book 1:3).

1. The Requirement of Obedience: *Slaves, be obedient to those who are your masters according to the flesh, with fear and trembling, in the sincerity of your heart (6:5).*

    Paul's instructions are to slaves and how they are to act toward those who are *masters according to the flesh.* The point will be made before we leave this passage that we all have another master who is according to the Spirit. A master according to the flesh has power only over the flesh, but a master according to the Spirit has power over everything, both flesh and spirit.

    Slaves are required by Paul to be obedient, not only when their masters are watching, but in sincerity of heart. This kind of obedience is to be real and heart-felt. It is to be internal and not merely external.

    It has been noted that the test of true faithfulness is what you do when no one is looking. That is a faithfulness that comes from the inside out and which does not depend upon someone looking over your shoulder.

2. The Representative of Obedience: *Slaves, be obedient... in the sincerity of your heart, as to Christ (6:5). With good will render service, as to the Lord, and not to men (6:7).*

Twice Paul says that the obedience of slaves to their masters is to be such that they are to consider their obedience really being toward Christ. It is as though obedience to an earthly master is to represent obedience toward Christ Himself.

This should not surprise us. Jesus told his disciples in Matthew 25 that the last judgment would see people being told with regards their treatment of the poor that *"to the extent that you did it to one of these brothers of Mine, even the least of them, you did it to Me" (Matthew 25:40).* Paul says the same thing here, that you will be judged not only for how you treat those who are needy, but also how you treat those who are in authority over you.

3. The Result of Obedience: *Knowing that whatever good thing each one does, this he will receive back from the Lord, whether slave or free (6:8).*

The principle of a reciprocal reward is a common theme to Scripture. Paul says in Galatians 6:7 that whatever a man sows, so he shall also reap. When you plant watermelon seeds, you can expect to harvest watermelons.

Paul applies that same principle to those who are slaves. They are called to live obediently, not only because it will result in a reward from their earthly masters, but because it is the Lord who is the final arbiter and who gives us our ultimate reward.

We are able to take this same principle today and apply it to the workplace, to home life, and to every area in which we are also called to be under authority. We are to live in a manner that reflects our assurance that it is the Lord who is the ultimate rewarder of our actions.

INSTRUCTIONS TO MASTERS

And masters, do the same things to them, and give up

threatening, knowing that both their Master and yours is in heaven, and there is no partiality with Him. (Ephesians 6:9).

Paul's opening words to the masters of slaves are quite striking as he says, "Do the same things to them." To what things does he refer? He has been telling slaves to see their service toward their masters as that which is given to the Lord. Now he tells masters to do the same things to their slaves. They are to treat their slaves as they treat the Lord. Not only does this mean they would no longer mistreat their slaves, but it also means they were to avoid even the threat of such mistreatment – Paul says they are to *give up threatening*.

The Greek word here translated "master" is *kurios* (κυριος). It is the same word that is regularly translated "lord" when the New Testament speaks of the Lord Jesus Christ. The point is that we are all slaves and we all have a master. If you are a Christian, then your Master is Jesus Christ. If Jesus is not your master, then you have another master and his name is sin. Jesus Himself said that *everyone who commits sin is the slave of sin* (John 8:34).

Paul reminds us that we Christians have a heavenly Master and that *there is no partiality with Him*. What does this mean? It means that God does not play favorites the way men play favorites. It means that God is not impressed by such things as social status or fame or wealth. He does not have one set of standards for slaves and another for masters. He judges all equally and without favoritism.

A QUESTION OF APPLICATION

Slavery is no longer an issue in our western society. This brings us to a question of application. What are we to do with Paul's instructions to slaves and to masters? Is this passage to be relegated to a mere intellectual exercise or a historical anachronism?

I believe it appropriate to take the principles taught in this passage regarding slaves and masters and to apply them to the employee/employer relationship. There are some obvious differences in the relationships. Slaves in the ancient world had little recourse to remove themselves from their slavery while employees in a working situation are able to resign from their position and take a different job. But in spite of these differences, there are some parallels.

Christian employees ought to be known for their sincere obedience and willingness to do their best on the job in which they are employed. We do not work merely to obtain a paycheck, but as a part of serving the Lord. Paul has already established this principle earlier in this epistle when he instructed each believer to *labor, performing with his own hands what is good, so that he will have something to share with one who has need* (Ephesians 4:28). Our labor is to be seen as a service to others, not merely in order to receive a paycheck, but to serve because we have first been served by the One who came to perform the ultimate service on our behalf.

In the same way, Christian employers should also be known for their gracious consideration of their employees. The Christian model of leadership is our Lord who was a servant-leader.

SPIRITUAL WARFARE
Ephesians 6:10-20

This commentary was years in the writing, though it came together into its present format within a relatively short period. There was one exception and that is the section to which we now come. I came to the last portion of Ephesians and to these verses in particular and my writing ground to a halt. It was left unfinished for over a year. What was the reason? To this day, I am not entirely certain, but I suspect that it has something to do with the spiritual warfare to which Paul alludes in this passage.

Warfare is a fact of life. There have been few instances in history that have not seen war in one place or another. My own father was an officer in the United States Air Force and in the course of his career he flew fighters in three different wars. I grew up on military bases, though my own adult experiences were more related to fire fighting and the emergency conditions of a fire ground. In that setting, I have experienced the burning, the smoke, the explosions, and the screams of the injured in a virtual war against disaster.

Paul uses this image of warfare to speak of the experience of the Christian. We are involved in a spiritual conflict that goes back through the ages to the Garden of Eden when a smooth-talking serpent led mankind into open revolt against the Creator. Since that day, every member of the human race has been a participant in that conflict on one side or the other.

Bad things happen on a battlefield. That is in the very nature of warfare. It is for that reason that we should not be surprised to see bad things taking place in this world. Battlefields are dangerous places and the spiritual conflict taking place all around us means that we will face some of those dangers.

While a battlefield is a dangerous place, it can be made all the more dangerous if one does not recognize the danger. Imagine someone being on a battlefield without being aware that a battle is taking place. Our imaginary individual is out for an afternoon stroll, blissfully unaware that there are bullets whizzing by or that bombs are exploding all around.

THE NEED FOR STRENGTH

Finally, be strong in the Lord and in the strength of His might. (Ephesians 6:10).

Paul introduces this section with a call to be strong. I cannot read those words without thinking of the charge of Moses to Joshua in the closing chapters of the book of Deuteronomy. Three times in Deuteronomy 31, Moses tells Joshua to "be strong and courageous" (31:6, 7, 12). Accordingly, after the death of Moses, Joshua gives this same charge to the Israelites who are preparing to enter the Promised Land (Joshua 1:6, 7, 9, 18). The Israelites were to be strong because they were about to enter a period of intense combat. They were being sent in to take possession of a land.

We are given the same call today. We are not being sent into a small section of land in the Middle East. We are being sent out to the entire world. Our charge is to make disciples of the nations. Our aim is nothing less than global conquest. We shall see that the means of this warfare is not to be by the use of physical force, but through the preaching of the gospel. We have a message that changes lives.

Notice that the strength to which we are called is *in the Lord*. It is *the strength of His might*. This is a phrase that Paul has already used in this epistle. He spoke in Ephesians 1:19 of the surpassing greatness of God's power that is in accordance with the strength of His might. Paul goes on in that passage to show how that strength received its fullest manifestation in the resurrection of Christ from the dead (1:20). The strength of the resurrection is to be our strength for today. We can stand firm because our Lord and Savior has defeated death and has taken His seat at the right hand of the Father.

Martin Luther's famed hymn that begins, "A Mighty Fortress is Our God," goes on to say in one of its stanzas, "Did we in our own strength abide, our striving would be losing." The good news is that we can be strong in the Lord and in the strength of His might.

THE NATURE OF THE ENEMY

Put on the full armor of God, so that you will be able

to stand firm against the schemes of the devil. 12 For our struggle is not against flesh and blood, but against the rulers, against the powers, against the world forces of this darkness, against the spiritual forces of wickedness in the heavenly places. (Ephesians 6:11-12).

Paul gives a name to the enemy. He refers to him as the devil. The Greek term *diabolos* (διαβολος) describes one who is a slanderer. The same term is used in Titus 2:3 where older women are warned against being *malicious gossips*; someone has jokingly referred to the problem of she-devils in the church.

The devil is a slanderer, but her we find that he has more than one plan. We are called to stand firm against his schemes. His tactics and methodologies change in response to his targeted audience.

We are to put on the full armor of God. This injunction will be repeated in the next verse, but first Paul goes on to explain why such armor is needed. It is because we are facing a series of attacks. Our enemy is the devil. He is the architect of the plans that are against us. That tells us something about the nature of our enemy as well as the nature of the conflict. It is spiritual in nature.

Our Struggle Is Not Against...	*Flesh and blood*
Our Struggle Is Against...	*The rulers* *The powers* *The world forces of this darkness* *The spiritual forces of wickedness in the heavenly places*

It has been suggested that, when describing the opposition we face, there is a distinction made between earthly forces versus heavenly forces. This further contrast would look like this:

Earthly Forces	**Heavenly Forces**
Rulers	Powers

| World forces of this darkness | Spiritual forces of wickedness in the heavenly places |

Here is the point. There are both physical and earthly enemies and there are also spiritual enemies and they work together. We make a mistake when we think that all the problems of our world can be solved by bringing physical force to bear because the conflict goes far beyond the mere physical realm. That was the mistake made in the days of the Crusades. Our struggle is not confined to flesh and blood. There is more than meets the physical eye to the global conflict in which we find ourselves. The real rulers of this world are not limited those who sit in presidential palaces. There are world forces and there are also spiritual forces operating from behind the scenes and in another dimension and they are all at work in our world.

A CALL TO STAND FIRM

> *Therefore, take up the full armor of God, so that you will be able to resist in the evil day, and having done everything, to stand firm. (Ephesians 6:13).*

For the second time, Paul calls his readers to take up the full armor of God. The phrase "full armor" is translated from the single Greek word πανοπλία (*panoplia*). It is a compound word made up of the joining of two words: παν (*pan*), "all," and ὅπλον (*hoplon*), "shield." This latter word is where the Greeks derived their term "hoplite" to refer to their armored soldier. The picture is of a soldier taking up all of his armor and readying himself for battle.

Throughout the last three chapters of Ephesians, Paul has made reference to the walk of the Christian. Starting from Ephesians 4:1 where he implored his readers to walk in a manner worthy of their calling, he has continued to urge them to walk in a way that befits their position in Christ. But now the image has changed. Now he tells them, not to walk, but to stand.

The call to stand firm in such a context brings to mind the image of soldiers in a battlefield formation. The battle would inevitably go to the army whose soldiers were able to stand firm and not break in the face of the enemy charge. They are to hold their ground in the face of an ongoing attack.

A DESCRIPTION OF THE ARMOR

> *Stand firm therefore, having girded your loins with truth, and having put on the breastplate of righteousness, 15 and having shod your feet with the preparation of the gospel of peace; 16 in addition to all, taking up the shield of faith with which you will be able to extinguish all the flaming arrows of the evil one. 17 And take the helmet of salvation, and the sword of the Spirit, which is the word of God. (Ephesians 6:14-17).*

Paul now moves from the instructions to the Christian soldier to a description of the armor that is to be worn by such a soldier. There are six points to this description:

The Image	What it Represents
Girded Loins	Truth
Breastplate	Righteousness
Shod Feet	Preparation of the Gospel of Peace
Shield	Faith
Helmet	Salvation
Sword	Word of God

From where does Paul derive this imagery? It is certainly true that he was well acquainted with the attire of the typical Roman soldier. He had been arrested by Roman soldiers and even now was in the custody of Roman officials. We can imagine his writing these words and glancing over to a nearby Roman guard in full array whose duty it was to watch over him.

At the same time, we should note the similarity of Paul's language in this passage with the words of the Old Testament prophet Isaiah. If Paul was familiar with the garb of the Roman soldier, he would have been at least as familiar with the words of the Old Testament prophets.

> *And He saw that there was no man,*
> *And was astonished that there was no one to intercede;*

Then His own arm brought salvation to Him,
And His righteousness upheld Him.
17 He put on righteousness like a breastplate,
And a helmet of salvation on His head;
And He put on garments of vengeance for clothing
And wrapped Himself with zeal as a mantle. (Isaiah 59:16-17).

Isaiah describes the coming of the Messiah. He dons the breastplate of righteousness and the helmet of salvation. This is striking, for Paul uses exactly the same description of this armor that is to be worn by the believer. The implications are obvious. The armor that we are to wear is not our armor; it belongs to Christ.

1. Truth: *Stand firm therefore, having girded your loins with truth (6:14).*

    We don't speak much today of girding your loins. The language hearkens back to the days when men wore long, flowing robes. Such dress styles worked well in the warm Mediterranean climate except when there was a call to action. At such a time, those long, flowing robes could become a hindrance and so, those robes would be gathered under a belt. Here that belt is used to represent truth.

    This same sort of imagery was used by the prophet Isaiah when he described the coming Messiah, the shoot from the stem of Jesse in whom would rest the Spirit of the Lord.

    > *But with righteousness He will judge the poor,*
    > *And decide with fairness for the afflicted of the earth;*
    > *And He will strike the earth with the rod of His mouth,*
    > *And with the breath of His lips He will slay the wicked.*
    > *5 Also righteousness will be the belt about His loins,*
    > *And faithfulness the belt about His waist. (Isaiah 11:4-5).*

    While Isaiah used the picture of the girding belt to represent righteousness and faithfulness, Paul uses that same image to represent truth. He has already described the Christian as one who speaks the truth in love (Ephesians 4:15) – we noted how the Greek text more literally speaks of how we are to be "truthing in love." He went on to say in Ephesians 4:25 that we are to lay aside falsehood and speak truth to our neighbors. We Christians should be known as people of truth. It should undergird everything we do and everything we say. This includes speaking truly about ourselves.

One of the most common charges we hear today about Christianity is how the church is full of hypocrites. This ought not to be. A hypocrite, by definition, is someone who says one thing and who does another. A fundamental part of our Christian message is that we are sinners who, apart from Christ, commit very real sins and who are so bad that we needed God's only Son to come and to die in our place the death we deserved. Thus, if we tell the truth about ourselves, no one ought ever to charge us with hypocrisy.

2. Righteousness: *Having put on the breastplate of righteousness (6:14)*.

We have already noted that the figure of *the breastplate of righteousness* is taken from Isaiah 59:17 where the Lord Himself is pictured as the one putting on righteousness as a breastplate. This suggests to us that the righteousness the Christian is to don is not his own righteousness; it is a righteousness that has been provided him by the Lord. We have been credited with the righteousness of Christ so that we are reckoned as being perfectly right in the eyes of God and, on that basis, we are justified – declared to be just and right.

It seems to me that Paul's description of the Christian putting on the breastplate of righteousness includes this fact of the imputation and reckoning of Christ's righteousness, but is not limited to that idea. The Christian is also called to live in a righteous manner as befits the position to which he has been assigned. God declares him to be righteous through faith, but then God also calls him to live righteously in the world. Paul told his readers in Ephesians 4:24 that they were to *put on the new self, which in the likeness of God has been created in righteousness and holiness of the truth*. A part of putting on that new self is putting on the breastplate of righteousness.

3. The Preparation of the Gospel of Peace: *Having shod your feet with the preparation of the gospel of peace (6:15)*.

Once again, we can turn to the prophet Isaiah for the source of Paul's imagery. Once again, the prophet is speaking in the context of a Messianic prophecy. This time it is taken from Isaiah 52.

> *How lovely on the mountains*
> *Are the feet of him who brings good news,*
> *Who announces peace*
> *And brings good news of happiness,*
> *Who announces salvation,*
> *And says to Zion, "Your God reigns!" (Isaiah 52:7).*

We see Paul's use of the familiar term "gospel" and should remember that it literally refers to "good news" and, as such, is the same term that is found in the Septuagint reading of the Isaiah passage.

The reference to the feet does not speak of the gospel, but more specifically, to the preparation of the gospel. The context of Isaiah's prophecy is helpful here as it also emphasizes the one who brings the good news and who announces God's salvation. This is a reference, not just to the gospel, but to the readiness of the Christian to share the gospel with others.

While it is true that the Lord has gifted some people in the area of evangelism, we are all called to bear witness of the truth of the gospel and to share that good news with others.

Paul has been using the analogy of a soldier and it is in such a context that we ought to see this reference to feet being shod with the preparation of the gospel of peace. We are called to a peace mission. It is our duty to take an offer of peace to a world at war. The peace that we offer is twofold. It is peace with God and it is also the peace of God.

The gospel involves making peace with God. That presupposes that mankind is not currently experiencing peace with God. To the contrary, the world today is at war with God. We have a ministry of reconciliation. We are peace envoys calling for nothing less than personal surrender to the God of the universe. The good news is that such a surrender will lead to peace with God. But it does not stop there. Once we have peace with God, it is possible to experience the peace of God. One can live in the midst of the conflicts of this world and experience a perfect peace.

4. Faith: *In addition to all, taking up the shield of faith with which you will be able to extinguish all the flaming arrows of the evil one*

(6:16).

In 1ˢᵗ Thessalonians 5:8, Paul calls his readers to *put on the breastplate of faith and love*. Both then and now, faith is described in the terns of defense as both a breastplate and a shield were defensive in nature. In this case, he goes on to describe how our faith *will be able to extinguish all the flaming arrows of the evil one*.

We are under attack and our primary defense in the midst of that attack is our faith. When we fall into sin, one of the things that has taken place is a lapse in our faith. If we really believed that sin is as bad as the Bible teaches it to be, then this would serve as a deterrent to sin.

At this point, we must give a warning. It has become increasingly popular today to speak of the importance of faith without any thought as to the object of that faith. People seem to think that it does not matter what you believe as long as you believe something. Nothing could be further from the truth. Having faith in faith is as barren as being in love with love or having money that you spend only on the accumulation of more money. T. J. Campo gives the following illustration.

Imagine that you see me packing up for a trip. You ask me, "Where are you going, John?" I reply, "I am going on a trip to the desert. In fact, I'm getting ready to take a hike through the Sinai Desert."

You check over my provisions. You see that I have a tent and plenty of sun screen. There is a coat for the chilly nights and there is a compass so that I won't go around in circles. There is only one thing I seem to be missing. What about water? "I've thought of that," I reply, and I pull out a tin cup. There is only one problem. The cup is empty. There is no water in it. "But that is okay," I insist, "I have my cup"

Faith is like that empty cup. Faith alone will not accomplish anything. If faith is to be effective, it must be in a proper object. What goes into the cup is the important thing. Our faith must be rooted in the reality of God's saving grace or else it is worse than useless, for it will give a false sense of security.

5. Salvation: *And take the helmet of salvation (6:17).*

Paul returns again to the words of the Old Testament from Isaiah 59:17. We have already noted that it is a Messianic passage and that this helmet of salvation come from the hand of the Lord. Paul uses this same image in 1 Thessalonians 5:8 where he speaks of a our helmet being the hope of salvation. This brings up an important question because when we speak of a hope, it is necessarily unrealized. I do not hope for something that I already possess. Is salvation a present possession or is it a hope. The answer is that it is both.

Paul has already described salvation is the past tense. He did so in Ephesians 2:8 when is said that believers have been saved by grace through faith. This salvation is an accomplished fact; it has taken place in the past with continuing results. But salvation also has a future tense. We have been saved, but we are still awaiting the fulness of that salvation. We look forward to the day when our condition will match our position; when our actual experience will match that which God has declared us to be.

Which is in view here? I would suggest that we are to see both in this passage. We are to hold to that which Christ has done on our behalf and we are also to hold to that which He promises to do in us in the future.

6. The Word of God: *And the sword of the Spirit, which is the word of God (6:17).*

Up to this point, the entirety of Paul's description has been given over to defensive armaments. You don't go attacking someone with a belt or a breastplate or sandals or a shield or a helmet. You wear or carry these devices because they aid in your defense. But now there is a change. For the first time, Paul makes mention of armament that is used

> Normally when Paul speaks of the Scriptures as the word of God, he uses the Greek phrase ὁ λογος του θεου (*ho logos tou theou*). But when we read in Ephesians 6:17 of the sword of the Spirit, which is the word of God, it is a different term for "word." Instead of λογος (*logos*), it is ῥημα (*rhema*). While some have sought to tie this in with the reference to prayer in verse 18, this is not necessary as Paul has already used ῥημα in Ephesians 5:26 when he spoke of the church being "cleansed by the washing of water with the *word*."

for the purposes of an offensive attack. It is the sword.

As we have seen with so many of these other analogies, this image also is taken from the pages of the prophet Isaiah. Once again, the prophet is speaking of the Messiah, the Servant of Yahweh, who would be sent to accomplish the mission of the Lord.

> *Listen to Me, O islands,*
> *And pay attention, you peoples from afar.*
> *The LORD called Me from the womb;*
> *From the body of My mother He named Me.*
> *2 He has made My mouth like a sharp sword,*
> *In the shadow of His hand He has concealed Me;*
> *And He has also made Me a select arrow,*
> *He has hidden Me in His quiver.*
> *3 He said to Me,*
> *"You are My Servant, Israel,*
> *In Whom I will show My glory." (Isaiah 49:1-3).*

Notice that the mouth of the Messiah is described as being *like a sharp sword*. The Septuagint uses the term μαχαρια (*macharia*) and Paul follows suit in this passage. Isaiah sees the future Servant of the Lord as the instrument who would bring about the Lord's ultimate work in the world. His words would be like a sharp sword in that they would be striking and to the point. The writer of the Epistle to the Hebrews uses this same analogy when he says that the word of God is alive and powerful and sharper than any two-edged sword. The book of Revelation captures this same symbolism when it portrays the coming of Christ, picturing Him with a sharp two-edged sword coming from His mouth (Revelation 1:16; 19:15).

As we conclude this mental picture, we should point out the corporate nature of the description. The command to take up arms is not given to a solitary individual, but to the entire church. If you read through this description and come away with a mental picture of a single soldier adorned in armor, you have the wrong picture. Each of these commands is given in the plural. We do not have a single soldier described here, but an entire army. This is a call to arms for the entire church.

The implications are obvious in light of what Paul has already said about the need for unity. Believers can only win the spiritual battle if they stand firm together, supporting one another. We stand in a battle line and we necessarily depend upon one another as a part of this formation.

THE CALL TO PRAYER

> *With all prayer and petition pray at all times in the Spirit, and with this in view, be on the alert with all perseverance and petition for all the saints, 19 and pray on my behalf, that utterance may be given to me in the opening of my mouth, to make known with boldness the mystery of the gospel, 20 for which I am an ambassador in chains; that in proclaiming it I may speak boldly, as I ought to speak. (Ephesians 6:18-20).*

As Paul moves to the subject of prayer, he has not really changed topics. He is still dealing with the topic of spiritual warfare and he comes now to that aspect of spiritual warfare that is central. There can be no victory in the spiritual conflict in which we are engaged without prayer.

1. The Universality of the Command: *With all prayer and petition pray at all times in the Spirit, and with this in view, be on the alert with all perseverance and petition for all the saints (6:18).*

    Within the space of this single verse, Paul makes four uses of the word "all." This repetition is deliberately striking and calls for our attention.

    - All prayer and petition
    - Pray at all times in the Spirit
    - Be on the alert with all perseverance and petition
    - Prayer for all the saints

    When Paul calls for all prayer and petition, he is pointing out that we are not limited to one type of prayer. We make a mistake when we think that there is some magical formula by which we should pray and never deviate from that formula. There are a host of prayers we can pray. Certainly the Lord's prayer is a good beginning, for that establishes a basic pattern for prayer. But our prayers should not be limited to the Lord's prayer. The Lord has given to us an entire book of prayers in the Psalms. You have not really begun to pray until you have prayed your way through the Psalms.

Our prayer is to be at all times. That means that while it is good and profitable to set aside specific times of prayer, it is also good and needful to pray throughout the day whenever opportunity arises. Paul says that such prayer is to be "in the Spirit." I take this to mean that we are to rely upon the Spirit when we pray and that we are to pray in such a way that our prayers reflect that which the Lord Himself would pray – to pray with His love, His concern, His passion, His desires.

Our prayers are to be with all perseverance. There will be times when we do not feel like praying. Pray anyway! There will be times when we feel as though our prayers are bouncing off the ceiling. Pray about your lack of faith! Prayer is a wake up call to your spiritual life.

Finally, prayers are to be made for all the saints. Notice the lack of self-centeredness in this command. We are to be in the business of praying for others. Our prayers of petition should not merely be for our own concerns, but rather for the concerns of the entire church. That does not mean we cannot also pray for ourselves, for we are part of the entire church for which we are to pray. Paul makes this clear when he asks that prayers be made on his own behalf.

2. The Specific Nature of Paul's Personal Request: *Pray on my behalf, that utterance may be given to me in the opening of my mouth, to make known with boldness the mystery of the gospel (6:19).*

Paul asks for the opportunity and the boldness to speak the mystery of the gospel. He has expounded upon that mystery earlier in this epistle. He has spoken of that which was hidden in former times but which now has been revealed, that the Gentiles have become fellow heirs of the promise of life through faith in Christ.

Paul wants the church to pray that he will accomplish that to which he has been called. I believe we are to pray in the same way. We should pray that we fulfill our calling.

3. The Position from which Paul Speaks: *I am an ambassador in chains; that in proclaiming it I may speak boldly, as I ought to speak (6:20).*

Paul is a prisoner of Rome. He describes himself as *an ambassador in chains*. He represents the God of the universe, but he does so from a position of outward humility. Yet he does not ask that his readers pray for his release. He is content with his current position. He asks only that he might fulfill his mission by speaking with a holy boldness as befits his position as an ambassador of Christ.

FINAL FAREWELLS
Ephesians 6:21-24

The last four verses of the epistle serve as closing comments and final farewells. The main body of the epistle is now complete. Paul has said what he wants to say. But there are a few final notes and closing comments. They come in the form of a word of commendation for Tychicus and a closing benediction.

NEWS FROM TYCHICUS

> *But that you also may know about my circumstances, how I am doing, Tychicus, the beloved brother and faithful minister in the Lord, will make everything known to you. 22 I have sent him to you for this very purpose, so that you may know about us, and that he may comfort your hearts. (Ephesians 6:21-22).*

We are not given a great deal of information about Tychicus. He is mentioned both here as well as at the end of the epistle to the Colossians and he seems to have been instrumental in carrying both these epistles to their particular destinations. We should remember that the Roman postal system was reserved for official documents and that private correspondence had to be hand carried. Thus Tychicus was sent by Paul for the express purpose of delivering these epistles.

Tychicus was coming home after an extended time of ministry with Paul. Acts 20:4 says that he was from Asia, a reference to the area we know today as the country of Turkey. He and a number of others had been with Paul on his third missionary journey and he had evidently been with Paul during at least a portion of his imprisonment. This is not the end of his ministry. He will be seen again in two of Paul's pastoral epistles (2 Timothy 4:12 and Titus 3:12).

Paul describes him as *the beloved brother and faithful minister in the Lord*. The reference to him being a "faithful minister" can be rendered a "faithful deacon" since the term deacon refers to a servant or a minister. While this does not necessarily mean that Tychicus held the particular office of a deacon, it is possible that he did. He seems to have played a vital role in Paul's ministry team and he reminds us that deacons play a vital role in the life of the local church.

He is being sent to Ephesus carrying this letter as well as to give a face to face report of Paul's situation, but also that he might comfort the hearts of the people there. This brings up a question. Why was such comfort necessary? Could not the people of Ephesus be comforted by reading Paul's epistle to them? Tychicus is bringing them Paul's epistle, but there is also a sense in which he will be Paul's epistle to them. He is going to exhibit the very sort of Christian walk to which they have been called in this epistle.

This tells me something about Christian leaders, whether they be pastors or elders or deacons. Christian leaders as to lead by what they do and not merely by what they say. They are called to lead by exemplifying Christian living. Tychicus is going to be an encouragement to the Ephesians both by what he says as well as by his presence among them.

CLOSING BENEDICTION

> *Peace be to the brethren, and love with faith, from God the Father and the Lord Jesus Christ. 24 Grace be with all those who love our Lord Jesus Christ with incorruptible love. (Ephesians 6:23-24).*

These final words in the epistle form a closing benediction. They also take us back to see what has been the overriding message of the entire book. This has been a book about peace, love, and faith.

Paul related in chapter 2 how Christ established peace, not merely between God and men, but also between Jew and Gentile, bringing both together in the unity of the Spirit in the bond of peace. In Ephesians 6:15 he spoke of the necessity of having feet shod with the preparation of the gospel of peace. The message of the gospel is a message of peace.

This has also been an epistle filled with love. The love with which we have been loved is one that began before time and Paul has related how it was in love that we were predestined to adoption as sons (Ephesians 1:4-5). His prayer for them has been that they might know the love of God that surpasses knowledge (Ephesians 3:19) and that they might walk in that same love (Ephesians 5:2).

Finally, this has been an epistle of faith. For the first three chapters, Paul's only command was that they might believe the good news of what Christ had accomplished on their behalf. We are saved through faith (Ephesians 2:8) and have our confident access to God through that same faith (Ephesians 3:12). Paul's prayer for the Ephesians was that Christ might dwell in their hearts through faith (Ephesians 3:17) and his goal for them was that they attain to a unity of the faith (Ephesians 4:13).

The closing verse of these epistle has been variously translated, not because the words themselves are difficult, but because the word order is such that it is not entirely clear what is to be the connection.

NAS	Grace be with all those who love our Lord Jesus Christ with incorruptible love.
NET, NIV	Grace be with all of those who love our Lord Jesus Christ with an undying love.
ESV	Grace be with all who love our Lord Jesus Christ with love incorruptible.
Greek Text	ἡ χάρις μετὰ πάντων τῶν ἀγαπώντων τὸν κύριον ἡμῶν Ἰησοῦν Χριστὸν ἐν ἀφθαρσίᾳ.

While all of these are possible, each of these translations take the term incorruptible (also rendered undying) to describe the love that we have for Christ. The problem is that the Greek text does not necessarily link these together and it is equally possible and perhaps even preferred to link this term, not with those who love, but with our Lord Jesus Christ. A literal rendering would read: *Grace be with all those loving our Lord Jesus Christ in immortality.*

The point that Paul is making is not that our love is so pure or incorruptible or undying, but that the One who we love is Himself the immortal One and those who love Him share in that same immortality. This brings us full circle to the opening words of Paul in this epistle where we saw the One who blessed us with every spiritual blessing in Christ.

*Blessed be the God and Father of our Lord Jesus Christ, who has blessed us with every spiritual blessing **in the heavenly places** in Christ... (Ephesians 1:3)*	*Grace be with all those loving our Lord Jesus Christ **in immortality** (Ephesians 6:24)*

Paul ends his epistle in the same place that he began his epistle. He ends with our position in the heavenly places, our realm in Christ in immortality. Throughout this epistle, he has called us to see who we are in the heavenlies and, on that basis, how we are to live here on earth.

BIBLIOGRAPHY

Barclay, William
1976 *The Letters to the Galatians and Ephesians: Revised Edition.* Philadelphia, PA: Westminster Press

Boice, James Montgomery
1998 *Ephesians: An Expository Commentary.* Grand Rapids, MI: Baker

Cheung, Vincent
2004 *Commentary on Ephesians.* Boston, MA: Vincent Cheung

Clark, Gordon H.
1985 *Ephesians*, Jefferson, MD: Trinity Foundation

Colin Brown (ed.).
1978 *The New International Dictionary of New Testament Theology in 3 Volumes.* Grand Rapids, MI: Zondervan

Constable, Thomas L.
2009 *Notes on Ephesians.* Garland, TX: Sonic Light

Dunnam, Maxie D.
1982 *Mastering the New Testament: Galatians, Ephesians, Philippians, Colossians, & Philemon.* Dallas, TX: Word.

Epp, Theodore W.
1977 *Living Abundantly: Studies in Ephesians.* Lincoln, NE: Back to the Bible

Foulkes, Francis
1974 *The Epistle of Paul to the Ephesians: An Introduction and Commentary.* Grand Rapids, MI: Eerdmans

Gabelein, Frank
1981 *The Expositor's Bible Commentary.* Grand Rapids, MI: Zondervan

Hendriksen, William
1989   *Galatians and Ephesians*. Grand Rapids, MI: Baker

Hodge, Charles
1860   *A Commentary on the Epistle to the Ephesians*. New York, NY: Robert Carter & Brothers

Hoehner, Harold W.
2002   *Ephesians: An Exegetical Commentary*. Grand Rapids, MI: Baker Academic

Lloyd-Jones, D. Martyn
1984   *Life in the Spirit in Marriage, Home, & Work: An Exposition of Ephesians 5:18 to 6:9*. Grand Rapids, MI: Baker

MacArthur, John Jr.
1986   *Ephesians*. Chicago, IL: Moody

McGerr, Patricia
1965   Johnny Lingo's Eight-Cow Wife. *Woman's Day Magazine*, Nov. 1965

Moulton, Harold K.
1978   *The Analytical Greek Lexicon*. Grand Rapids, MI: Zondervan

Robertson, Archibald Thomas
1931   *Word Pictures in the New Testament*. 6 Vols. New York, NY: Harper & Brothers

Stott, John W.
1979   *The Message of Ephesians*. Downers Grove, IL: InterVarsity Press

Utley, Robert James
2005   *Paul Bound, the Gospel Unbound: Letters from Prison*. Marshall, TX: Bible Lessons International

www.ingramcontent.com/pod-product-compliance
Lightning Source LLC
Chambersburg PA
CBHW081345040426
42450CB00015B/3313